JOAN BLAEU and his GRAND ATLAS

by

Dr. Ir. C. KOEMAN

Professor of Cartography, State University of Utrecht

Published in the United Kingdom and the Commonwealth, excluding Canada

by

GEORGE PHILIP & SON LIMITED

LONDON

in cooperation with

THEATRVM ORBIS TERRARVM LTD

AMSTERDAM

ISBN 90 221 1080 X
Printed in The Netherlands

Contents

Acknowledgements

Nos. 7, 8, 18, 19 by courtesy of the Municipal Archives, Amsterdam; No. 11 of Ir. A. Baron van Styrum, Heemstede; No. 12 of the Rijksmuseum, Amsterdam; Nos. 14, 21, 22 of the Universiteitsbibliotheek (University Library), Amsterdam; Nos. 16, 17 of the Nederlandsch Historisch Scheepvaart Museum (Maritime Museum) Amsterdam; No. 24 of Mr. G. L. Berk, Nederhorst den Berg; No. 25 of the Museum Meermanno Westreenianum, The Hague.

Illustrations

Preface

Joan Blaeu's *Grand Atlas* reflects many aspects of the social and intellectual life of Holland in the 17th century, the era that is known in history as the Golden Age, the Golden Age of the young Republic of the United Netherlands.

The contents of this unprecedented atlas illustrate the high standards of contemporary cartography and geographical knowledge, and its presentation bears witness to the superb craftsmanship of engraver, printer, binder, and papermaker. The production of the vast atlas is a demonstration indeed of the enterprise of the Amsterdam printers of the time and of the financial and commercial capacity of the House of Blaeu in particular.

It would be an overstatement, however, to say that the elegant and sumptuous *Grand Atlas* was typical of every walk of life in 17th-century Amsterdam. The costly atlas was in fact exclusively designed for those members of the patriciate who could command both the material and the intellectual resources that were needed to buy it and to appreciate it. Apart from its artistic aspects in which a broad stratum of Dutch society participated, the Golden Age was actually experienced as such by a relatively small circle of privileged persons in the world of trade and industry. In the immediate vicinity of incredible wealth the beautiful city of Amsterdam harboured a vast majority of the less fortunate who had practically no share in the felicities of life in a golden age. This was a social structure that was by no means confined to Amsterdam or the Dutch Republic, and its shortcomings were indeed more pronounced in other European cities. Yet we would do well to realize that this 'monument of the grand life in the Golden Age of Holland' (as the *Grand Atlas* has been entitled) originated in an era in which plagues, catastrophes, wars, famine, and crime were part and parcel of everyday life. Art and science, trade and industry flourished at a time when life was short and uncertain, but with an urgency about it that was unique to the period.

The Dutch achievements in various fields in the Golden Age often seem incredible, especially if we consider the limited resources that were available. The production of the *Grand Atlas* or, to use the standard Latin title, the *Atlas Maior* was one of these significant achievements. The enterprise involved problems of such magnitude in matters of planning and personnel, of financial investment and the recruiting of specialists, that any modern publisher would be glad to acknowledge the superiority of the man who was active three hundred years ago, Joan Blaeu. He must have been inspired by a creative impulse that sent him riding roughshod over the carefully calculating business methods we consider indispensable, consciously aspiring to achieve a culmination in atlas production such as the world had never seen before. And to what end? It is difficult to find an adequate answer. It could not have been for reasons of commercial profit alone, since the risk was too great with the enormous investments involved. Nor for social reasons such as the provision of employment, for planned economy was an unknown concept at the time. This stupendous productivity can be explained to a certain extent as the logical outcome of the tendency, already manifest in the previous three decades, to enlarge the world atlas. An impetus may also have been provided by the rivalry in the field of atlas production between the houses of Blaeu and Janssonius. But a definitive explanation should probably be sought in less concrete motives such as prestige and display — considerations which were indeed prevalent at the height of Amsterdam's prosperity and power. It must have seemed absolutely imperative to create something that would astound the whole civilized world, something that would be worthy of the 'Empress of Europe'.

1-2. Printer's marks of the Blaeus.

Prior to 1612, Willem Blaeu appears to have had no printer's mark of his own. After that date he used a mark representing a balance with a terrestrial globe in the right scale pan and a celestial globe in the left, below it the word 'Praestat'. A new mark was devised after 1621 which was subsequently used by all members of the family: a globe flanked by the figures of Time on the left and Hercules on the right, with the device 'Indefessus agendo'. Sometimes, especially in smaller publications, we find the globe without figures and device.

3

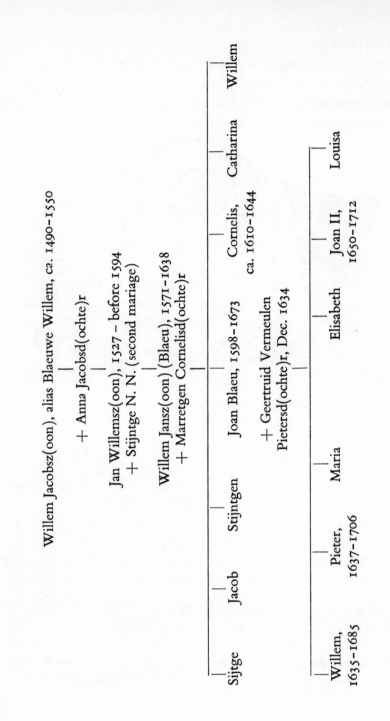

Willem Jacobsz(oon), alias Blaeuwe Willem, ca. 1490–1550

+ Anna Jacobsd(ochte)r

Jan Willemsz(oon), 1527 – before 1594
+ Stijntge N. N. (second mariage)

Willem Jansz(oon) (Blaeu), 1571–1638
+ Marretgen Cornelisd(ochte)r

Sijtge   Jacob   Stijntgen   Joan Blaeu, 1598–1673   Cornelis,   Catharina   Willem
                                                         ca. 1610–1644

+ Geertruid Vermeulen
Pietersd(ochte)r, Dec. 1634

Willem,   Pieter,   Maria   Elisabeth   Joan II,   Louisa
1635–1685 1637–1706   1650–1712

1. Biography of Joan Blaeu

There is very little documentary evidence concerning the children of Willem Jansz(oon) Blaeu. At least seven children were born of his marriage to Marretgen (Marretie) Cornelisd(ochte)r of Uit-geest. The eldest, Joan, was born at Alkmaar in 1598 or early 1599. References to his date of birth show several discrepancies. He is recorded three times in the *Album Studiosorum* of the University of Leiden, in each case with the indication 'Alcmari-anus': on 11 May 1616 as 17 years old, on 8 June 1617 as 18 years old, and on 3 March 1618 as 20 years old (this should probably read 19). His age is recorded in a notarial deed dated 9 March 1653 as fifty-four. Elias[1] mentions that Blaeu was born on 23 September 1596, which seems unlikely.

Willem Jansz apparently moved to Amsterdam in 1599, where he set up as a globe- and instrument-maker. In a request for a license submitted to the States of Holland on 5 August 1608 he mentions his rapidly growing family. We know practically nothing about Joan's early years except that he was a student at Leiden from 1616 to 1619(?). The poet Pieter Cornelisz Hooft wrote to Jacob Wytz about Joan Blaeu in a letter dated 1 July 1634 in the following terms: 'He is an intelligent and educated young man, a relative of mine. His father, Willem Blaeu, a philosopher and a pupil of Tycho Brahe's, is well known and could even have been famous had he wished.'

Joan's first home in Amsterdam was the new house built on the property purchased by the elder Blaeu on 5 November 1599 on 'De Lastage, aan de Waelkant' in the dockyard area situated just beyond the mediaeval ramparts in the north-east quarter of the town. In 1605 the family probably moved to the house 'op 't Water', now the west side of the street known as Damrak, where Willem Jansz opened his shop and first printing-press at the sign 'in de Vergulde Sonnewijser' (sub signo deaurati). To distinguish his establishment from those of other booksellers 'op 't Water' (Johannes Janssonius from 1618 onwards, Jacob Aertsz Colom from 1624 onwards), Willem Jansz added 'bij de oude Brugghe' (near the Old Bridge) to his imprint.

It was here on the waterside that Joan Blaeu spent his childhood. The environment in which he was reared was decidedly not limited in its interests. Apart from the maritime publications, his father produced works in the field of literature and art at his press. Willem Jansz was tolerant in religious matters and did not condone the repression of the Roman Catholic faith.

Joan Blaeu's parents probably belonged to the Remonstrant persuasion (as a few theological books printed by Willem Blaeu seem to indicate), but Joan himself later gave evidence of sympathies with the Roman Catholic faith. This raises some tricky problems, since Roman Catholics were not admitted to many public offices. The following arguments can be cited in support of the thesis that Joan Blaeu did indeed sympathize with Roman Catholicism in his later years:

— The printing of missals, produced by the Jesuits, for the foreign market, which were usually sold under the imprint of Cologne publishers.[2]

— The publication of the Italian town atlases, with the *Civitates Status Ecclesiastici* appearing as the first volume in 1663 with a dedication to Pope Alexander VII signed by Joan Blaeu.

After his student days at Leiden, the young Doctor of Law presumably went on the traditional grand tour of Europe as was customary for sons of wealthy parents. This would have been in 1620. Ten years were to elapse before we meet Joan Blaeu as printer and map-maker. Nothing is known about his activities in the interim. No documents have survived to show whether he had in any way been a useful member of society. He did not marry until he was thirty-five, which gives us reason to suppose that he must have been well satisfied with his carefree bachelor existence at his father's expense.

Joan presumably went into partnership with his father in or about 1630. In several maps in the *Appendix Theatri Ortelii et Atlantis G. Mercatoris* of 1631 the names of father and son appear in a joint imprint. The preface of the first edition of the *Novus Atlas* (German text, 1634) is likewise signed by Willem and Joan Blaeu. The name of his brother Cornelis only appeared in the imprint of work published after the death of the father in 1638. The partnership of the two brothers, however, was of short duration, Cornelis apparently dying young, presumably before 1644.

It is remarkable that the output of atlases increased considerably after Joan's marriage in December 1634. There is no justification, however, for assuming that it was only owing to the fortuitous circumstance of his father's death that the leadership of a large printing-house devolved on Joan Blaeu. The following facts refute such an assumption:
a. After the death of Willem Blaeu in 1638 the press, established just the year before on Bloemgracht, continued to be run in an exemplary manner.
b. The spectacular development of the atlas *Theatrum* received its greatest impetus in the period 1638-1640.

c. Joan Blaeu was appointed map-maker to the Dutch East India
    Company as his father's successor immediately after the latter's
    decease.
The last argument in particular convinces us that he must have
been an active and competent cartographer before 1638.

The period 1638-1650 was one of tremendous progress for the
city of Amsterdam and the Republic. There were spectacular
developments in the political situation with regard to the war
with Spain and in the economic situation. The trade with Asia
and the Americas brought great prosperity to Amsterdam, and in
its wake the arts and sciences flourished as never before. These
material and cultural advances were reflected in Blaeu's greatest
publishing project – the expansion of the *Theatrum* from two
volumes in 1635 to six volumes in 1655 – and also in the production of countless books, maps, and globes of monumental proportions.

The letters of this great master printer which have been preserved afford an insight into the conduct of his life and affairs. He
maintained an extensive correspondence with scholars, authorities, and businessmen all over Europe, writing in Latin, French,
or Italian, well-formulated and courteous missives to the great,
brief and business-like letters to the smaller fry.

The printing business paid Blaeu handsome dividends. Yet his
career was by no means meteoric. It was relatively late in life that
he achieved the status of the wealthy patrician who was eligible
to high office. Dr. Joan Blaeu held several public offices. From
1651 to 1672 he served on the City Council without a break,
acting as alderman in 1651. Elias (q.v.) mentions his appointment
as Captain of the Civic Guard in 1650 and 'Overman' of the
Handbow Archers' Guild in 1651, as commissioner of fortifications in 1655 and of the ammunition magazines in 1659. The

period in which he was active as a regent of Amsterdam coincided with the Stadholderless regime. Prince William II had died on 6 November 1650. Amsterdam, where the Republican or States faction flourished, opposed the prince in the internal political strife and his last action against the recalcitrant city had been the siege of 30 July 1650. After this incident the influence of Amsterdam was greatly strengthened particularly in the States of Holland. It was in this period that Joan Blaeu was elected to the Council.

He was therefore involved in various ways in the economic, cultural, and political life of his times: by virtue of his membership of the Council, his office of cartographer to the East India Company, and his connexions with artists and scholars. To illustrate the facets of his versatile life we reproduce a representation of the attributes of a mid-century patrician statesman and soldier in a painting by one of the great Dutch masters of the Golden Age: Govert Flinck's portrait of Gerard Hulft[3], secretary of the city of Amsterdam, who exchanged his soft seat in the Council Chamber for the hard life of an officer in the field and who was appointed Councillor and Director-General of the Dutch East Indies in 1654. He had been a colleague in office of Joan Blaeu and was ultimately killed in action at Colombo in 1656 during hostilities with the Portuguese in Ceylon. The attributes depicted on the painting could have served equally well as symbols of Joan Blaeu's activities: globe, drawings of fortifications, dividers, compass, astrolabium, cross staff, quadrant, books, bills, etc. In later life Joan Blaeu was also moved by the desire to gather in his share of the enormous profits that were to be reaped in the new colonial empire. He turned his attention to the plantations in North America. A notarial contract of 1663[4] exists whereby Joan Blaeu, Willem van Meekeren, Gerrit Arentsz Suyck, Hans Hontum, and Willem Hontum commit themselves to engage in trade and cultivation 'in the islands of Virginia', the associates undertaking to supply the negroes for the plantations. Here we find Joan Blaeu in the unexpected role of slave-trader!

By this time Joan Blaeu had turned over a share in the business to his son Pieter. On 7 March 1662 he applied to the civic authorities for permission to hold a public sale of the stock in his book-shop 'op 't Water'⁵, announcing at the same time the transfer of the shop and part of the stock to his son Pieter. It must have been quite a considerable sale as witnessed by the size of the catalogue: — Catalogus librorum omnium facultatum et variarum linguarum, quospublica auctione venales exponet Joannes Blaeu, die Iunii & seqq. Amstelaedami, Apud Joannem Blaeu, MDCLXII. (Copy in the Harvard Library B. 1935 5.216, and in the Kongelige Bibliotek [Royal Library], Copenhagen). It comprises the following sections: p. 3-64 Libri Theologici, p. 1-31 Libri Juridici, p. 1-19 Libri Medici, p. 1-54 Libri Miscellanei, p. 1-26 Livres Francois, 27-32 Libri Italici, 33-36 Libros Espanoles, p. 1-8 Nederduytsche Boecken, p. 1-24 Hochteutsche Bücher.

Glory and prosperity are never permanent, but the misfortune that befell Joan Blaeu was completely unexpected. Well advanced in years, he was still active in his business and working on the further expansion of his *Atlas Maior*, with the last volume of the Spanish edition in the press, when disaster struck on all sides. His Gravenstraat press was destroyed by fire and shortly afterwards he was relieved of his office on the Council.

The year 1672 was fraught with disaster for the country. In the resultant turmoil the Orangists gained influence throughout the Commonwealth, even in the Council of Amsterdam. The country found itself at war with France, England, Münster, and Cologne, and under the stress of circumstances the Prince of Orange was elevated to the Stadholderate (William III). With feelings running high against the anti-Orangist magistrates, there were serious disturbances in Amsterdam and elsewhere. Acting on emergency powers from the States, the new Stadholder dismissed sixteen anti-Orangist members of the Amsterdam Council on 10 September. Joan Blaeu was one of them. The vacancies were filled by supporters of the Prince. Blaeu was deeply distressed by his dismissal, coming as it did after the loss of his press in the fire of 22 February in the same year. These reverses may possibly have been responsible for his subsequent decline of health and on 28 December 1673 he died. Epitaphs by Gerard Brandt and Joost van den Vondel allude to the disillusionment under which this great son of Amsterdam must have laboured in the last year of his life:

De wijze Blaau, zoo wijdt vermaart,
Die 't hemels ront, die zee en aard'
In zijnen druk toonde op 't papier,
Bestreden door het felle vier,
En door de vaale Nijdt vertreen,
Wordt minst gedrukt van deze steen.
Gerard Brandt

Hier sluymert Blaeu, gedrukt van dezen kleinen steen,
Al 't aertrijk door bekent,
Hoe quam hij aen zijn endt?
De gansche werrelt viel dien grooten man te klein.
Joost van den Vondel

GEOGRAPHIE,

QVI EST

LA PREMIERE PARTIE

DE LA

COSMOGRAPHIE
BLAVIANE,

EN LAQVELLE

LA TERRE

EST REPRESENTÉE

DANS DES CARTES

ET

ILLVSTRÉE DE DESCRIPTIONS.

A AMSTERDAM,
Chez **JEAN BLAEU.**
MDCLXIII.

3. Title page of the first volume of Joan Blaeu's *Grand Atlas*, 1663.

3. Printing-house
and cartographical institute

The reader of this introduction to the facsimile edition of the *Grand Atlas* might easily forget that Joan Blaeu was more than a printer of atlases. The reverse is rather the case; in addition to his large output of books Joan Blaeu also produced an international atlas in several languages. From 1620 to 1638 his father had already printed numerous books on his press(es) in the premises 'op 't Water'. The enormous growth of his business, however, made expansion necessary. It is reasonable to conjecture that Joan Blaeu was the driving force behind the plans to expand the printing house.

In 1637 the printing office removed from the original site 'op 't Water' to larger premises on Bloemgracht. The number of presses was increased to nine and a typefoundry was installed. The House of Blaeu was probably the largest press of Europe at the time. It was certainly the most up-to-date and for this reason attracted many foreign visitors. Willem Blaeu is believed to have introduced several important improvements to the current 16th-century models of the printing-press. Lloyd Brown describes the improvements as follows[6]:

'In 1683, Joseph Moxon summed up the situation in these words: There are two sorts of presses in use, viz. the old fashion and the new fashion, the new fashion being Blaeu's press.

The improvements in the new fashion were simple enough, but no one had thought of them before, small details that made a big difference and tended to eliminate chronic backache as an

4. Engraved portrait of Willem Jansz. Blaeu, 1571 -1638.

5. Map of Europe, from Blaeu's *Atlantis Appendix*, 1630.

SCVLPTVRA IN ÆS.

Sculptor noua arte, brassteata in lamina   Sculpit figuras, atque prælis imprimit.

6. Interior of a map-printing house. Engraving by Philip Galle.

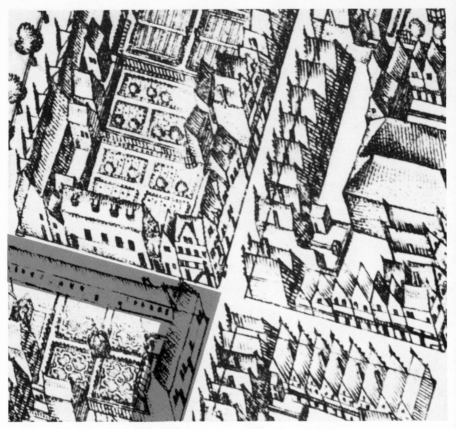

7.   The printing house on Bloemgracht, opened in 1637. Detail from the plan of Amsterdam by Balthasar Florisz. van Berckenrode, 1647.

7a.   One of the many 'cartouches' in the *Grand Atlas*.

occupational disease of printers. In a very few years Blaeu's improved printing press was standard equipment in Europe, and was reluctantly accepted by English printers who were at first skeptical.'

The following description of the printing house of the Blaeu's on Bloemgracht is derived from Philip von Zesen's *Beschreibung der Stadt Amsterdam* (1664). It appears from the preface that in 1663 Von Zesen had been resident in Amsterdam for twenty-two years and that he had acquired citizenship there in 1662.

'On the Bloemgracht, at the third bridge and the third by-lane, stands the world-famous printing house of Mr. Joan Blaeu, councillor and alderman of this city. The establishment is equipped with nine presses for letterpress printing, called after the nine muses, and six presses for printing copper-plates, and also with a type-foundry.

The premises on the canal, together with the adjacent residence of the founder, has a breadth of 75 ft and extends 135 ft, or 150 ft if the house adjoining it at the rear is included, along the east side of the by-lane (which is likewise the property of said Mr. Blaeu). In front, facing the canal, is a room containing a number of cabinets in which are stored the plates which are used for the atlases, the Dutch and Walloon town atlases, and for the marine and other priceless books, which must certainly have cost a ton of gold. Next-door is the room where the copper-plates are printed; beyond it is the entry where, in the part flanked by the above-mentioned lane, they are wont to wash down the type after printing.

Then comes the printing office proper in a long gallery, well provided with windows on both sides. At the far end is a stock-room where the type and other materials used in printing are kept. Before this room is a staircase leading to a room on the next floor where the corrector reads the proofs and revises and marks

17

the errors made by the compositor. Here, too, there is a long ante-chamber or loft where, when the printing of the entire book is completed, the printed sheets are gathered into the order of appearance and also stored.

At the very top is a similar loft for the same purpose and at the far end of this, over the previously mentioned proofreader's room, is the foundry where type for printing in several languages is cast.

The foundation stone of this excellent building was laid in 1636 by Mr. Joan Blaeu's elder son Willem, and at a later date, on 13 September, the press was installed here.

The founder of the firm was the said Mr. Joan Blaeu's art-loving father Willem who had been a pupil of Tycho Brahe's for a considerable period, and a very diligent disciple indeed, for he modernized and improved and even invented many instruments for the advancement of astronomy, navigation, and other related sciences.'

In addition to nine presses for letterpress printing, the works was equipped with six presses for printing copper-plates according to Von Zesen. This figure seems incredibly small if we realize that Blaeu printed something like one million impressions from roughly a thousand copper-plates of maps and town-views within a span of four years (cf. chapter on *Atlas Maior*). Printing from copper-plates is a far more laborious process than letterpress printing and we would therefore expect the equipment to be proportionately more elaborate in the production of books containing an equal amount of plates and text.

Von Zesen does not mention an engraving department. This is hardly surprising, since it had always (from the 16th to the 19th century) been customary for engravers to ply their craft at home in their own workshops. In the chapter dealing with the printing of the *Atlas Maior* we have estimated that approximately eighty men must have been employed at the printing house.

A second printing house was opened in 1667 in Gravenstraat. The names 'Blaeu Erf' and 'Blaeustraatje' in this area still remind us of the site of the press. Most of the map printing was presumably done here. The account of the fire which destroyed the printing works on 22 February 1672 (q.v.) seems to justify this supposition. It records that 'copper-plates stacked in the far corners melted like lead in the flames'. The Gravenstraat establishment was also furnished with several presses for letterpress printing and large quantities of type.

Several famous Dutch books were printed at the press of the Blaeus, such as Hooft's *Historien* and Hugo Grotius's *Corpus juris* and *Annales et historiae de rebus belgicis* (1659). The *Corpus juris* acquired fame because the most scrupulous search failed to uncover a single printer's error in the entire voluminous work. The impeccable quality of the presswork was renowned far and wide and on the strength of it Joan Blaeu was appointed printer to King Gustavus Adolphus of Sweden.

When Von Zesen mentions the stock-room with 'the plates which are used for the atlases, the Dutch and Walloon town atlases, and for the marine and other priceless books', he is referring to the material from which the maps and illustrations were printed i.e. the copper-plates for the atlases and for the famous town atlases of the Netherlands (1649), for the *Flandria Illustrata*, (rights and plates of which had been purchased by Joan and Cornelis Blaeu from Henricus Hondius in 1641 for the sum of Fl. 11,000.—) and for Caspar Barlaeus's work *Rerum per octennium in Brasilia gestarum historica*, 1647. To these large folio editions were added in 1663 the three town atlases of Italy: *Citta del Vaticano*, *Roma*, and *Napoli & Sicilia*.

As manager of the largest printing house in Europe, Joan Blaeu frequently conferred with colleagues and businesmen from abroad. He regularly attended the Frankfurt Book Fair. Sometimes, however, he was represented by a foreign colleague, and we have evidence of this in an agreement between Joan Blaeu and Alexander Harttung drawn up by the notary Hendrik Venkel at Amsterdam on 17 March 1659[7]: 'Harttung will try to sell at the Frankfort Book Fair in the autumn of 1659 all kinds of books, globes, maps, etc. which Blaeu will send him. Harttung will participate in the sales for 1/3 part, paying Blaeu Fl. 1000,— before the autumn fair'. A similar contract with Harttung is dated 26 April 1662.[8]

By 1660, when his business had reached its zenith, Joan Blaeu's sales of printed pilot books had fallen to negligible proportions. Other Amsterdam printers and shipmerchants dominated the field. Next to Jacob Aertsz Colom, Anthonie Jacobsz, in partnership with his sons Casparus and Jacobus, had become an important dealer. Their ranks were swelled in 1650 by Pieter Goos and in 1659 by Hendrik Doncker.

Continuing in the tradition of his father Willem Jansz, Joan Blaeu was predominant as a globe-maker. Celestial and terrestrial globes in the standard formats of 10, 13, 24, 34, and 67 centimetres in diameter were produced in great numbers in his workshop. This lucrative business was carried on until far in the 17th century. As late as 1668 we find Joan Blaeu buying plates for the gores of a *globe celestis* from Johannes Janssonius van Waesbergen.[9]

Apart from these ready-made globes, a pair of globes of exceptional format were constructed on one occasion in Joan Blaeu's workshop. They were commissioned by the Syndics of the Dutch East India Company on behalf of Prince Crain Patengalo of Macassar.[10]

In 1644 the Prince requested from the Dutch East India Company authorities at Batavia the following curiosities in exchange for a cargo of sandalwood:

A large map of the world or mappa mundi, the text in Spanish, Portuguese or Latin language.

A book with the description of the entire world, or Atlas, in Latin, Spanish, and Portuguese with maps.

A pair of the best telescopes, giving a good view through metal tubes, light.

A fine large burning-glass.

12 pieces of triangular cut glass through which diverse colours can be seen in the air.

30 to 40 thin bars of iron.

A sphere mundi made either of brass or iron.

The Syndics in Amsterdam were immediately able to comply with part of this request. On 5 February 1648 the Prince of Macassar received a copy of Blaeu's large-scale map of the world with Spanish text, Blaeu's atlas in four volumes, and two telescopes and a burning-glass. The globes, however, were not immediately available owing to their exceptional size. A globe with a circumference of 157 to 160 inches (= c. 410 cm.) has a diameter of approximately 130 cm. Blaeu's largest standard globe measured 67 cm in diameter. The globe for the Prince of Macassar had to be specially constructed and drawn. Joan Blaeu was commissioned to do so by the Syndics of the Dutch East India Company who wrote on 2 September 1648:
'The Globus terrestris ordered for the Prince of Macassar is in execution . . . with this one person is constantly occupied, but the execution will take a year longer, however, than was estimated. It will be an exceptionally fine piece of work, the like of which has never been made before in this country or elsewhere. Having no doubt that it will be sent with the Company's fleet

ultimately in spring 1649 and that it will give satisfaction there, we shall hear about that in due time'.

In the minutes of the meeting of the Syndics on 13 December 1649 it is recorded that:

'the Messrs. Voet, Carpentier, and Munter are delegated by the meeting to go and view the large Globus terrestris commissioned from Dr. Johan Blauw for the Prince of Patanboe of Macassar and to report on it'.

And on 31 January 1650:

'the Delegates of the Company reported that they had spoken to Dr. Johan Blauw about the remuneration claimed by him for making a large globus terrestris, for which, subject to the approval of the meeting, he was promised five thousand guilders and ... 1200 for instruments ... used, which he will accept, and the aforementioned Delegates were thanked for their trouble'.

Though the prince had originally asked for a pair of globes, there was only mention of a terrestrial globe in the transactions. This globe was indeed dispatched to Batavia on 25 April 1650 surrounded by special precautions, and forwarded from there to Macassar on 13 February 1651 together with the bill of Fl. 11,592.30. Notwithstanding the high price, the prince decided to keep the globe. We know nothing further about the fate of this giant globe nor whether other specimens were made. Since the scale of the globe was 1 : 10 million, i.e. twice the size of Blaeu's largest standard globe, the gores would have had to be specially drawn. It seems unlikely that they were also engraved. This was presumably a manuscript globe but the records are not clear on the point. The covering letter sent from Amsterdam with the globe reads:

'By the *Oliphant* is dispatched the large globus terrestris commissioned for the Prince of Macassar a few years ago, packed in two cases and costing according to the bill Fl. 11,592.30. Travelling by the same ship is a second mate, Hendrick Jansz. Lutma van Yeperen by name, who is fully acquainted with the use of this globe and has been signed on especially for this reason; also dispatched is an Instruction drawn up by Dr. Jan Blaauw to understand the use of the same and as something of the kind has not been made before in this country, this should be carefully preserved and followed. We have acted in the foregoing on the advice of the Lords Seventeen'.

A similar giant globe was presented in the second half of the 17th century to the Czar Alexei Mikhailovich by the States-General of the Netherlands.[11] This specimen is now preserved in the Istoricheskiy Musey in Moscow. These large globes of Blaeu's probably inspired the Danish scholar Adam Olearius to construct what is known as the Gottorp globe. Peter the Great took this globe to Moscow in 1715. It was damaged by fire in 1747 and restored in 1778.[12]

Though the output of printed pilot books and printed charts had been considerably reduced and Joan Blaeu had undertaken no new initiatives in this branch since about 1640, his work as chart-maker to the Dutch East India Company became increasingly important.

Like his father who had succeeded Hessel Gerritsz as cartographer by a decree of 3 January 1633, Joan Blaeu filled the post of official map-maker to the Dutch East India Company, having been appointed as such on 22 November 1638. The duties of the Company's cartographer included the making of manuscript charts and sailing directions for the navigators of the Dutch East India Company and the verification of the journals kept on the voyages. Unlike the practice in his father's time, the entire map stock was kept at East India House. It was here that the now extremely rare rutters for the voyages to the East Indies were drafted.

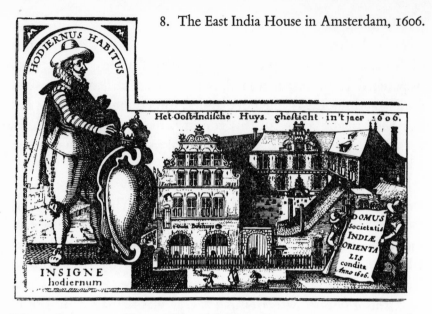

8. The East India House in Amsterdam, 1606.

Here, also, were the confidential files where, contrary to regulations, copies were made in 1660 or thereabouts for prominent private citizens like Laurens van der Hem. Joan Blaeu had probably been privy to these infringements of the regulations.

In his atlases Joan Blaeu made relatively little use of the information in the East India Company's files. The maps of Asia reproduced in the major atlas, for instance, were mainly printed from plates which already existed in 1635. The discoveries of Tasmania, New Zealand, and Kamchatka were incorporated in Blaeu's large-scale wall maps but the detailed charts of the Asian coastlines were never transposed into atlas maps. In the years around 1660 Joan Blaeu could easily have compiled a marine atlas surpassing anything that existed in the field (the marine atlases of Van Alphen, Doncker, Van Loon) had it not been incompatible with his office as chart-maker of the Dutch East India Company. A fundamental distinction should therefore be made between Blaeu's commercial cartographic activities such as atlases and wall

24

maps and his manuscript maps designed for the Dutch East India Company's navigators.

On the other hand, the above-mentioned marine atlases of Van Alphen, Doncker, and Van Loon (all of them appearing around 1660) did incorporate data deriving from the rutters of the Dutch East India Company. Their printed marine atlases therefore supplemented Joan Blaeu's printed cartographic *oeuvre* which lacked marine cartography.

It is normal publishing practice to distribute printed catalogues. Very little of such matter has unfortunately survived owing to its ephemeral character. This chapter concludes with a summary of the information at our disposal concerning the contemporaneous bibliography of the books, atlases, and maps of the Blaeus. These catalogues are the only documents we have giving us an insight into the range of Joan Blaeu's book and map production, since all the commercial correspondence and book-keeping records of the publishing house have been lost.

BIBLIOGRAPHIES OF BOOKS, MAPS AND ATLASES, PUBLISHED BY THE BLAEUS

A. A contemporary catalogue by a German author, listing maps published in the Netherlands shortly before 1670:
Simon Paulli, *Orbis terraqueus in tabulis geographicis et hydrographicis descriptio. Argentorati* [Strassburg]. In Officina Libraria Editoris, 1670. Copy in Leiden University Library. It was devoted to the work of the Blaeus, Janssonius and Nic. J. Visscher, and gives the contents of, i.a., the *Atlas Maior* of Joan & Corn. Blaeu and the *Novus Atlas* of Janssonius.

B. Beughem, Cornelius à, *Bibliographia mathematica et artificiosa novissima perpetuo continuanda, seu conspectus primus. Catalogi librorum mathematicorum . . ., quibus . . . sparsim suis locis in-*

seruntur mathematico-physicorum et physico-mathematicorum, arto-
ficiosorum et ad delectationem usumque viatae humanae conducentium
scriptorum specimina. Quotquot currente hoc semiseculo, id est ab
anno reparatae salutis MDCLI, per universam Europam in quavis
lingua . . . aut novi, (aut) emendatiores et auctiores typis prodierunt
. . . Accedit Cosmographiae sive Atlantis Majoris tam Blaviani
quam Janssoniani brevis conspectus harmonice exhibitus. Amstel-
odami, 1688.

In this work cross-reference is given between the maps of
Johannes Janssonius and those of the Blaeus.

C. A condensed bibliography of the Blaeu atlases is given by:
David Clement, *Bibliothèque Curieuse*, Göttingen, 1753. Vol.
IV, pp. 267-276.

D. Ample information on the atlases of Ortelius, Mercator,
Blaeu, in: E. G. Woltersdorf, *Repertorium der Land- und Seechar-*
ten, Wien, 1813.

So far we know of only six different publishers' catalogues by
the Blaeus and one (1661) referred to, but not traced. They are:

1633. *Catalogus Librorum Officinae Guilielmi Blaeu. Designans*
libros, qui tam ipsius typis & impensis prodierunt, quam quorum
alias copia ipsi suppetit. Amsterdami, Ex officina Guilielmi Blaeu,
1633. Copy in the Bibliothèque Mazarine, Paris.

1646. *Catalogus Librorum et Tabularum, Geographicarum et Hydro-*
graphicarum nec non, Spaerarum etc. Joannis Blaeu, Amsterledami,
Apud Joannem Blaeu, 1646. Copy in the Biblioteca Nazionale,
Vitt. Emanuele, Rome.

1659. *Catalogus librorum. Omnium facultatum & variarum liguarum,*
Qui in officina Ioannis Blaeu, . . . Amstelaedami Apud Joannem
Blaeu, 1659. Copies in Amsterdam University Library; Konink-
lijke Bibliotheek (Royal Library), Brussels; Kongelige Bibliotek
(Royal Library), Copenhagen.

1661? Brunet mentions a stock catalogue dated 1661 in which details of the various editions of atlases are mentioned. No copy known. (J. Ch. Brunet, *Manuel du libraire et de l'amateur de livres*, Ve ed. 1860. Vol. 1, col. 959).

(1670-71?). *Catalogue des atlas, théâtre des citez, globes, spheres, & cartes Géographiques & Marines, mis en lumière par Jean Blaeu, à Amsterdam demeurant op 't Water*. Copy in the Plantin-Moretus Museum, Antwerp.

1662. *Catalogus Librorum quos publica auctione venales exponet Joh. Blaeu, Amstelodami 1662*. Copy in the K.B. Copenhagen and in the Harvard University Library, Cambridge, Mass.

1674. *Catalogus Librorum variorum ... Joh. Blaeu, Amstelodami, 1674*. Copy in the Biblioteca Nazionale, Florence.

No doubt the number of catalogues issued by Willem Blaeu and afterwards by his son Joan Blaeu, must have been considerable. We might expect some twenty different lists of the publications of the Blaeus in the span of years between 1600 and 1674 (Joan Blaeu died in 1673). Only one book list issued by Willem Blaeu, of 1633, is known. As might be expected, it contains – apart from the sea atlases or pilot books – only the *Appendix* as an atlas published by Blaeu himself. But the atlases by Mercator-Hondius are also listed in this catalogue.

Of the other catalogues listed above, only those of 1646 and 1670-1671 are specifically map catalogues. Part of the catalogue of 1646 was repoduced in F. C. Wieder's *Monumenta Cartographica*, 1925-1933, pp. 77-78. The catalogue of 1659 has been analysed by W. Gs Hellinga in the booklet: *In officina Ioannis Blaeu*, Amsterdam, 1961.

The unique catalogue of 1670-1671, with French text, was mentioned in C. Koeman's *Collections of maps and atlases in the Netherlands*, 1961, p. 28, and was reproduced in facsimile for the first time by Theatrum Orbis Terrarum Ltd., Amsterdam, 1967.

Frontispiece of William Jones, Blean's The Light of Navigation 1612

3. Origin and growth of Blaeu's Atlas

Dr. Joan Blaeu's father Willem Jansz took to the publication of land atlases at a relatively late date. The first intimation we have of a plan to compile an atlas of the world appears in a letter of 1626 from Willem Blaeu to Sir John Scot.[13] But it was not before 1630 that the *Atlantis Appendix* containing 60 maps, 37 of them printed from plates which had originally belonged to Jodocus Hondius II, saw the light.

From 1606 to 1629 (death of Jodocus Hondius II) the large Mercator Atlas published by Hondius dominated the market and Willem Blaeu could hardly hope for success in this field as long as the Mercator Atlas enjoyed such popularity. His press was in fact working to capacity on his pilot books, the *Licht der Zeevaert* from 1608 onwards and the *Zeespieghel* from 1623 onwards. Until 1619 Willem Blaeu had had the monopoly of pilot books. In this year his neighbour and rival Johannes Janssonius issued an exact copy of *Het Licht der Zeevaert*. Another assault was made on Willem Blaeu's secure position in the field by the issue of an entirely new and original pilot book *De Vijerighe Colom* by Jacob Aertsz Colom. This touched Blaeu on the raw. He had to face the fact that his *Licht der Zeevaert* and *Zeespieghel* were no better than similar work published by other nautical publishers and that with the increase in shipping the competition in the trade would become even fiercer. It seemed sensible to cut down on pilot books and to concentrate on developing atlas cartography in a form that was not available elsewhere. Globe construction and the issue of separate maps continued to be a very profitable source of income.

The *Atlantis Appendix* was followed in 1631 by an *Appendix Theatri A. Ortelii et Atlantis G. Mercatori* with 98 maps. At the same time he was preparing for the publication of a large world atlas that was to surpass the atlas of Henricus Hondius. In this urge to outdo his rivals lies the germ of the impulse that was responsible for the creation of the *Grand Atlas*. The impulse by itself, however, could be no guarantee of success. A well-planned scheme for a truly original world atlas was at least as essential. Joan Blaeu presumably advised his father on these plans.

Willem Blaeu's intentions to publish an international edition of a new world atlas are recorded in a newspaper published at Amsterdam, the *Nieuwstijdingen bij Jan van Hilten*, on 11 February 1634. This fact is of sufficient importance to quote the text of the advertisement in full:

'At Willem Jansz. Blaeu's press in Amsterdam the large map-book or Atlas is currently being printed in four languages: Latin, French, German, and Dutch. The German edition will appear about Easter, the Dutch and French editions in the month of May or ultimately early June, and the Latin shortly afterwards. All editions on very fine paper, and brought up to date with newly engraved copper-plates and new detailed texts.'

That Willem Blaeu was unable to realize all his intentions in 1634 is evident from the date of issue of his atlases, viz. 1635. The chronological sequence of publication indicated by the prefaces is shown in the table on p. 26.

The extent of Blaeu's ambitions for a world atlas is revealed in the preface of the two-volume edition of 1635 in which Blaeu writes: 'It is our intention to describe the entire world, that is to say the heavens and the earth and the seas in several volumes like these two of which two more will follow shortly'.

But Willem Blaeu did not live to see the issue of the other two volumes he had prepared. These appeared in 1640 (Italy) and 1645 (England). And the promised description of the heavens and the seas never materialized at all. We therefore frequently find people adding a marine atlas (usually that of Pieter Goos) and a celestial atlas, the *Harmoniae Cosmographicae* of Andr. Cellarius (published by Johannes Janssonius) to the nine or twelve volumes of their *Atlas Maior*.

The publication of an 'international atlas' was a formidable enough task, however, even without a description of the heavens and the seas. This atlas, the *Theatrum Orbis Terrarum*, was issued in four languages, Latin, Dutch, French, and German, in the period 1635-1655 according to the table on pp. 38-39.

Joan Blaeu succeeded indeed in producing the most voluminous world atlas of all time. In 1635 he had already outdone his rival Johannes Janssonius, the two volumes of his *Theatrum* containing a total of 207 maps. The 1634 Dutch edition of the Mercator-Hondius-Janssonius atlas contained 182 maps and the 1636 English edition 195. Then Janssonius overtook his rival with the issue of his *Nieuwen Atlas* in two volumes in 1638 with 247 maps. The appearance in 1640 of the third volume of Joan Blaeu's *Theatrum* (with 62 maps of Italy), however, tipped the scales: three volumes of *Theatrum* totalling 273 maps. Joan Blaeu maintained his lead, being the first to issue a fourth volume (England) which contained 59 maps on 58 sheets, but Janssonius followed close on his heels with an issue of an England volume in 1646 comprising 62 maps on 56 sheets and even took a slight lead in 1650 with the issue of a fifth volume containing 33 maps in which the 'Waterworld' and the 'Antique World' were incorporated. Then Blaeu forged ahead, issuing his fifth (Scotland) and sixth (China) volumes in rapid succession in 1654 and 1655.

Joan Blaeu had surpassed his rival in Amsterdam as well as

publishers in other countries, who indeed never achieved a comparable output of atlases at any time in the 17th century. The six-volume atlas was certainly the most expensive that money could buy. Information about the price is supplied in a letter of 31 December 1655 from Joan Blaeu to Sir John Scot[15]: 'Atlas, 6 vols. bound 196 gulden, the same printed and bound 216 gulden. Vol. V of the atlas, bound, 25 gulden, the same printed and bound 36 gulden.'

Around 1620 Amsterdam had already acquired a paramount position in atlas cartography with the issue of the series of the Mercator-Hondius Atlas. But Joan Blaeu deserves the palm as originator of the encyclopaedic world atlas. The conception of this quite unprecedented and stupendous project was entirely his own. It was not till 1654 that an atlas comprising 100 maps was compiled in France by the geographer Sanson[16], which, albeit on other grounds, could be called remarkable. The display-loving European aristocracy, however, still showed a marked preference for the large six-volume atlases of Blaeu and Janssonius over the smaller, but scientifically superior French atlases.

The composition of Joan Blaeu's six-volume *Theatrum* showed a lack of balance that was mainly due to the addition of the Scotland volume with 49 maps and of the final volume, China' with 19 maps. The atlas doubtless took the prize for sheer bulk with these additions but according to our lights the presentation of these two countries received undue emphasis. A modern publisher would not dream of compiling a world atlas in which such excessive representation was accorded to countries with a limited sales potential. The inclusion of this material in the *Theatrum* was pure opportunism on the part of Blaeu. He was well aware of the fact that his clients were interested in quantity in the first place.

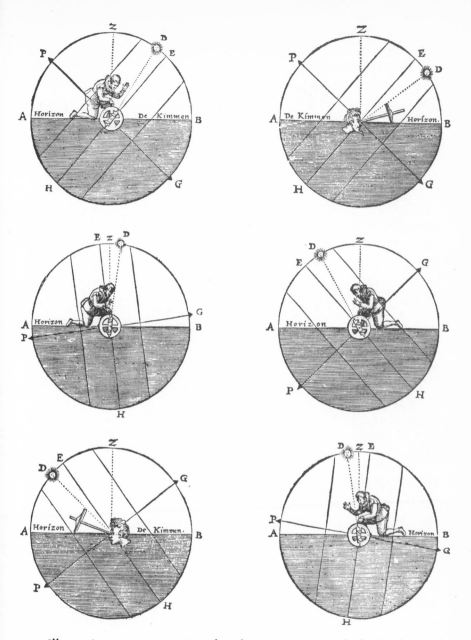

10. Illustrations accompanying the chapter 'How to finde the height of the Pole by the Sonne' in *The Light of Navigation*, 1612.

11. Joan Blaeu, 1598–1673. Portrait painted by J. van Rossum, 1663.

12. Gerard Hulft, secretary of the city of Amsterdam, colleague of Joan Blaeu, *c.* 1650-1654. Portrait painted by Govert Flink.

13. Map of the World, from Joan Blaeu's *Atlas Maior*, 1662.

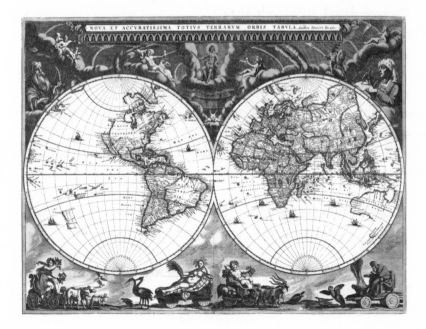

The Spanish edition of Joan Blaeu's *Theatrum* deserves special attention. No complete sets of a six-volume Blaeu atlas are known prior to 1656 but we have definite information that he had printed part of the Spanish *Theatrum* by 1657. In March 1657 Joan Blaeu wrote to Sir John Scot that the corrections suggested by him for the maps of Scotland would be incorporated in all future editions including the Spanish 'in which language I am now printing it' (the atlas).[17] Copies are known of the Scotland volume in Spanish with a licence dated 24 March 1659 and the pasted-on title curiously dated 1654. The England volume was likewise printed in 1659, that is prior to the actual issue of the Spanish *Atlas Maior*.

THE *Novus Atlas* OR *Theatrum Orbis Terrarum*

German text 1634 1 vol. (see Wieder's description[14])

German text 1635 2 vols. Preliminary essay, one volume smaller. Preface dated 10 March 1634.

German text 1635 2 vols. Final edition comprising two volumes. 109 and 99 maps resp.

Dutch text 1635 2 vols. Preface dated 22 April 1635. 104 and 103 maps resp.

Latin text 1635 2 vols. Preface dated 'ipsis Idibus Aprilis'. 105 and 102 maps resp.

French text 1635 2 vols. Preface dated 1 July 1635. 105 and 103 maps resp.

THE DEVELOPMENT OF THE *Theatrum Orbis Terrarum* AFTER 1635 (see table on p. 38-39)

1638 Before 1638 a supplement containing 24 maps must have been issued, as such an *Appendice* was incorporated in an issue of the French edition of 1638. This supplement appeared as an appendix to the third volume (Italy) of the French, Dutch, and Latin editions. Of the four editions the French was developed first of all.

1640 A third volume (Italy) was published, first with French text, followed in the same year by an edition with Latin text. The publication of a fourth volume was pending, as is demonstrated by a small supplement containing four maps of the British Isles that was added to the third volume of the Latin and French editions.

1642 The small supplement of the British Isles was now also added to the German and Dutch editions of the third volume. These third volumes appeared for the first time in 1642.

1645 The fourth volume (England) was published for the first time with French and Latin text. The prefaces are dated 1 October 1645 and September 1645 respectively.

1646 A Latin variant of the fourth volume with its preface dated September 1645 issued in 1646, followed by the German edition, preface dated 1 March 1646, and finally the Dutch edition dated on the titlepage 1646 but with a preface dated 12 November 1647.

1640-1650 Volumes I, II, III, IV reprinted in the four versions, Latin, Dutch, German, French as demonstrated in the table.

1654 Volume V was issued in the four versions. The prefaces in the Dutch, Latin, and French editions are dated 10 June 1654; the preface of the German edition is dated 16 June 1654.

1655 Volume VI was issued in its four versions with the prefaces all dated the same day. In each edition four privileges are given dated 7 January, 20 March, 16 April, and 11 May respectively.

1655-1658 Variants of volumes I, II, and III with Dutch and French text appeared c.1658. Variants of the second and third volumes with Latin text appeared in 1655.

French text Volume						Latin text Volume					
I	II	III	IV	V	VI	I	II	III	IV	V	V
1635	1635					**1635**	1635				
1638/40											
	1640	**1640**				**1640**	**1640**	**1640**			
	1640	1640						1640			
		1640									
		1640									
						1641/41					
1642											
1643/44						1643					
	1644	1644				**1644/45**					
1645	1645	1645	**1645**			1645	**1645**	**1645**	**1645**		
										1645	
			1646								
1647	1647	1647									
			1648							**1648**	
1649/50						1649					
						1649/55					
1647/50	1650	1650					1650	1650			
				1654							**1654**
					1655		1655	1655			I
1658	1658	1658									

Bold type: new edition. Otherwise: variants

Dutch text Volume						German text Volume					
I	II	III	IV	V	VI	I	II	III	IV	V	VI
						1634					
5	1635					1635	1635				
						1635	1635				
						1638					
						1641/42	1641				
2	1642	1642					1642	1642			
2	1642	1642									
	1642	1642									
		1643					1643				
									1645/46		
									1646		
7			1646/47			1647	1647	1647	1647		
			1646/47								
			1648			1648		1648	1648		
						1649/47					
0	1650	1650									
		1650									
				1654						1654	
					1655						1655
9/58	1658	1658									

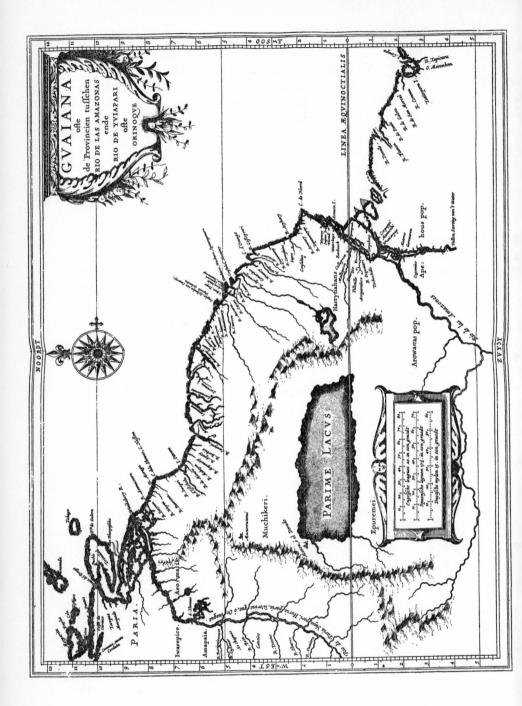

4. The Atlas Maior

The renown of Joan Blaeu's *Atlas Maior* was not primarily based on the high standards of scholarship in the maps and text. It was rather the superb typography, the beauty of the six hundred hand-coloured maps, and notably the unrivalled size that made the atlas desirable. Patricians of the period had a propensity for pompous display, not least in their libraries, and in this respect Blaeu's *Atlas Maior* suited their often rather snobbish tastes very well. The customers demanded heavy paper, large format, and luxury bindings.

The atlases were obtainable from the printer in the 'ordinary' Blaeu binding i.e. yellow vellum with a modest gilt tooling which included the printer's mark of the Blaeus. Luxury bindings in morocco leather or purple velvet were specially made on commission. Such luxury bindings have come down to us with the coats of arms of the original owners tooled in gold. These costly and artistic bindings were made, for instance, by the great Amsterdam binder Albert Magnus from about 1660 to 1680. An owner desiring a further embellishment of his atlas would commission an illuminator to overlay the prints in gold and colour with the finest materials available. One of the most renowned of these illuminators was Dirck Jansz van Santen, who was also employed by the lawyer Laurens van der Hem to decorate his atlas which, now known as the Eugene Atlas, is preserved in the National Bibliothek in Vienna.

In the 17th century Blaeu's *Atlas Maior* was a traditional gift presented on behalf of the United Republic to royal and other personages. In 1688 the Sultan of Turkey received a copy. Admiral Michiel de Ruyter was presented with a copy in 1660 in commemoration of his victory in the two-days battle against England. A presentation copy to the emperor Leopold II, bound in purple velvet and with the dedication illuminated in red and gold, is now in a private library in the United States. The *Atlas Major* frequently also featured as a present on trade and diplomatic missions of the Dutch East India Company and the States-General. We have mentioned earlier how a copy of Blaeu's *Theatrum* was sent to the Prince of Macassar. The Dutch even went to the lengths of honouring a notorious Barbary pirate with a Blaeu atlas, one volume of which, the Town Atlas of the Netherlands, has been preserved. It is described in a sales catalogue of Frances Edwards, London (1930?):

Special Dedication Copy from the States General to Syde Abdalla ben Sydi Muhamed, Prince of Salé, and no doubt one of the gifts of a contemporary Dutch Embassy who favoured an alliance with that Prince against Spain. The dedication to Sydi Muhamed is printed in Dutch and Arabic and curiously asks for God's blessings on that rapacious corsair.

In maritime Holland the absence of a marine atlas in the Blaeu series must have been felt as a serious omission, but is was one that Blaeu was unable to redress. Owners of a large Blaeu therefore frequently added the *Zeeatlas ofte Waterwereld* (1666) of Pieter Goos to their atlas in a uniform binding. Sometimes the series was further expanded with the town atlases of Italy and the Netherlands and with the *Atlas Celestis* and *Atlas Antiquus* of Janssonius to form a set of sixteen or even twenty volumes. An *edition de luxe* of this type is to be found in the Nederlands Historisch Scheepvaartmuseum, the maritime museum in Amsterdam. The magnificently bound atlas was not seldom kept in a beautifully carved display cabinet with glass doors, specially made for this purpose, such as the specimen in the Amsterdam University Library.

PRINTING

The planning involved in printing the three editions of the *Atlas Maior* (Latin, French, Dutch) within a span of three or four years exceeds the range of our imagination. We are inclined to consider 17th-century book production as a primitive and laborious process, but if we analyse the work actually performed, we find that we have to revise this opinion.

In the following we give an estimate of the time required for the composition, printing, and binding of the three editions of the *Atlas Maior*, assuming a relatively small impression of 300 copies in each edition. We had to impose this limit, since it was evident from our calculations that a larger impression would have been impossible with the actual capacity of the press. We have also confined ourselves to maps with text printed on the reverse. The size of the letterpress impression presumably ranged from 500 to 1000 copies per leaf. (The copper-plate was invariably printed after the letterpress).

To calculate the composition time we must first examine the text pages of the *Atlas Maior*. We find the text arranged in two columns of approximately 55 lines, set in a 10 to 13 point type. The length of the lines is 10 cm.

A hand-compositor spends an average of four minutes on a line. This results in $4 \times 55 \times 2 = 440$ minutes per page. If headings, etc. are added, we can assume a total setting time of eight hours for one page of the *Atlas Maior*. The next step is to count the number of text pages. The Latin edition of the *Atlas Maior* comprises approximately:

Vol. I: 210 pp. of text	Vol. VII: 344 pp. of text
Vol. II: 272 pp. of text	Vol. VIII: 218 pp. of text
Vol. III: 329 pp. of text	Vol. IX: 258 pp. of text
Vol. IV: 260 pp. of text	Vol. X: 262 pp. of text
Vol. V: 400 pp. of text	Vol. XI: 287 pp. of text
Vol. VI: 220 pp. of text	

This results in a total of 3000 text pages on 1525 folio-sheets. In the French and Dutch editions there are only slight deviations, so that roughly 10,000 pages of text had to be set and 5000 sheets printed all told in the three editions. Composition, therefore, required 80,000 hours or, with a productive capacity of 10 hours per day, 8000 days (The time required for proofing, distribution of type, etc. must be added to this). It must have been a full-time job for eight compositors to achieve this gigantic undertaking within three years (= 1000 working-days).

Blaeu had nine printing-presses in operation on which 300 × 5000 = 1,5 million sheets had to be printed in letterpress (2,5 million for an impression of 500 copies). Assuming a printing speed of 50 sheets per hour, the total will be 30,000 hours or, if the nine presses were running simultaneously, over 3300 shop-hours i.e. 330 working-days of 10 hours. It seems highly improbable, however, that all nine presses would have been in operation for that length of time on the *Atlas Maior* to the exclusion of all other work.

The time required to print the copper-plates can be estimated as follows: with an output of 300 copies, the approximately 600 map plates must be printed 3 × 600 × 300 = 540,000 times. At a rate of 10 impressions per hour, this results in a total of 54,000 hours on six presses or 9000 hours in the entire department, i.e.

900 working-days of 10 hours if the copper-plate department was working to capacity.

The amazing thing, however, is that when the production of the *Atlas Maior* was in full swing in 1663, Joan Blaeu was also busy completing his town atlases of Italy. These comprised 148 engravings and over 730 pages of text. We must assume, therefore, that Blaeu had more than six presses at his disposition for printing copper-plates or that he had the work executed at other houses. The fact that he later, in 1667, proceeded to install presses for copper-plate printing in his second establishment in Gravenstraat points in this direction.

The next stage is the binding. In atlas production this is an extremely laborious process which involves the mounting of each sheet on a guard. Our experience with a similar procedure in the facsimile edition of the *Grand Atlas* of 1967 and 1968 taught us that with modern, but not mechanical, methods approximately 100 maps can be guarded per hour. About 700,000 sheets of letterpress and maps required guarding. This would have taken something like 10,000 hours and we estimate the length of the entire operation, i.e. including the binding, at 300 days if 3 binders were employed.

To sum up: the total production time of the three editions of 300 copies each of the major atlas with uncoloured maps, issued in 1662, 1663, and 1664 was:

composition	1000 working-days	8 compositors
letterpress printing	330 working-days	9 presses
copper-plate printing	900 working-days	6 presses
binding	300 working-days	3 binders

In this estimate no attention was paid to:

a. the German edition *Atlas Maior dasz ist Weltbeschreibung* of 1667, as this had been compiled from sheets printed for the six-volume *Novus Atlas*.

b. the Spanish edition of the *Atlas Maior*, part of which consisted of sheets printed c.1654-1662 and part of sheets printed after 1662. This means that it was not till after publication of the Latin, French, and Dutch editions that Blaeu could find time to complete the Spanish edition.

c. the colouring of maps, which preceded binding. A part of every edition was preserved in unbound sheets, since customers frequently wished to employ their own binders.

With the information at our disposal we are able to calculate the number of men employed in Blaeu's printing office. With nine presses running non-stop, Blaeu must have employed 25 compositors. Letterpress printing would require 20 pressmen and copper-plate printing 12. Adding 5 proof-readers, 10 assistants, 3 binders, and 5 type-founders, we came to a total of 80 men in the Bloemgracht establishment. This number can indeed be accommodated in a two-storey building with a floor-space of 25 × 50 metres.

PRICES

Blaeu's *Atlas Maior* was the most expensive printed book that money could buy in the latter half of the 17th century. The prices are quoted in the 'Catalogue des Atlas, Theatre des Citez. . . Par Jean Blaeu' of 1670 (?)[18]:

Atlas en François en XII Volumes, illumniné & relié doré
 sur la couverture & sur la tranche   fl 450
Le mesme comme dessus, mais point illuminé   fl 350
Atlas en Latin XI Volumes, illuminé & relié, doré sur la
 couverture & sur la tranche   fl 430
Le mesme comme dessus, mais point illuminé   fl 330

Atlas Espagnol est sous la presse & aura xii ou xiii
   Volumes, dont les dix sont achevés, et se vendent illu-
    minés & reliés, dorés sur la couverture & sur la tranche fl 460
Le mesme comme dessus, mais point illuminé   fl 390

Lors que les autres Volumes jusques au nombre susdit seront faits,
se vendront successivement, à mesure que chacun sera achevé.

Touts les Atlas susdits sont reduits en ordre, auquel ils demeu-
ront, sans que cet ordre sera jamais changé, & tous ont les mesmes
cartes, à la reserve de celuy en Espagnol, lequel estant achevé, sera
si accompli que les autres.

The catalogue distinguishes between coloured and uncoloured
copies. The binding was included in the price. There was a difference of Fl. 100,— in the price of coloured and uncoloured copies.
As a twelve-volume atlas comprises approximately 600 maps, this
is equivalent to 15 cents or three 'stuyvers' apiece. These figures
should be related to contemporary cost of living. In the years
1660 to 1680 prices went up. In 1660 or thereabouts an assistant in
the book trade earned about two guilders (Fl. 2,—) a week. The
rent of a bookshop was anything from Fl. 400,— to Fl. 700,— a
year. To transpose the price of a twelve-volume Blaeu atlas into
our time, we must use a multiplication factor of approximately
100, which means that a modern atlas with 600 maps would now
cost Fl. 45,000.—. Approaching the question from another angle,
we may say that a twelve-volume Blaeu atlas selling today at
Fl. 45,000.— has not decreased in actual value even if we leave its
historical interest out of account.

When the bookshop and printing house of Blaeu closed down,
the *Atlas Maior* continued to be in demand. It frequently turned
up at public book sales where it fetched high prices. To cite a few
examples:[19]

1. Book collection of Cornelis Nicolai, sold in Amsterdam in 1698. The *Atlas Maior*, the Dutch and Italian town atlases, the *Atlas Celestis* and *Atlas Maritimus* of Janssonius, together 21 volumes for Fl. 910.—

2. Book collection of Paulus van Uchelen, sold in Amsterdam in 1703. 'A very remarkable Atlas of Blaauw on the largest format paper, very tastefully illuminated . . .' for Fl. 400.—

3. On the same occasion Hendrik Wetstein sold by auction at Amsterdam nine bound and three unbound sets of the major atlas which fetched between Fl. 300.— and Fl. 400.— each.

In the mid-18th century an economic recession sent the prices down, a *Grand Atlas* of 1663 only fetching Fl. 90.— in 1749. Th. Georgi's *Europ Bücher Lexicon*, Leipzig, 1742 lists: Atlas Major Blavianus, xi vol.: 127 Thaler. In the 18th and the 19th century prices dropped still lower. In Fred. Muller's catalogue *Neerlande-Russe* of 1859 (no. 981) the 1663 *Grand Atlas* is quoted at Fl. 65.—.

BIBLIOGRAPHY

The edition with French text or 'Le Grand Atlas'
The French edition, comprising twelve volumes, is literally the most voluminous of all editions. It contains five maps more than the Latin edition and one less than the Dutch. The French edition, moreover, was the only one that went into a second edition. All volumes of the first edition are dated 1663. The dedication to Louis xiv is dated 1 January 1663.

The volumes of the second edition are all dated 1667. Part of the text was reset, but only volumes vi (Scotland) and xi (Asia) show major differences with the first issue.

Locations: *1st edition, 1663*: University Library of Amsterdam. This copy, with the presentation inscription to Colbert, Minister

48

of Finance to Louis XIV, has been used for the facsimile edition.

Bibliothèque Nationale, Paris, G 31-42; Library of the Berchmanianum College, Nijmegen; B.Naz., Rome; A. H. de Vries Collection, University of California, Berkley; James Ford Bell Collection, Minneapolis; National Bibliothek, Vienna; Bibliothèque Royale (Royal Library), Brussels; Kongeliçe Bibliotek (Royal Library), Copenhagen; Saltykov Public Library, Leningrad; L'Arsenal, Paris; Chambre des Députés, Paris.

2nd edition, 1667: Bibliothèque Nationale, Paris, X.f. 13; British Museum; Library of Congress, 479; Joh. Enschedé & Zonen, Haarlem; Boston Public Library; Bibliothèque Publique & Universitaire, Geneva; Bibl. Czart, Cracau.

The edition with Latin text

This edition was the most widely sold. The volumes are all dated 1662. The dedication to the emperor Leopold II is dated 9 June 1662. The presentation copy, bound in purple velvet, is in the Mellon Library, Upperville, Virginia. A reprint of the first volume is dated 1665.

Locations: Nine copies in the Netherlands in i.a. University Library of Amsterdam, Koninklijke Bibliotheek (Royal Library) at The Hague. Eight copies located in Italy. Further copies in: British Museum; Library of Congress; Bibliothèque Nationale, Paris; Royal Library, Copenhagen; Saltykov Public Library, Leningrad; University Library, Ghent; Plantin-Moretus Museum, Antwerp; University Library, Wroclau.

The edition with Dutch text

The edition with Dutch text comprised only nine volumes and would consequently have been rather less expensive than the other editions. It is not mentioned in the catalogue (1670) which was exclusively destined for foreign use. The volumes are not all dated alike. Volumes I, II, and III are dated 1664. Volume IV is dated either 1648 or 1662, Volume v is dated either 1654 or 1662. Volumes vi and vii are undated, volume viii is dated 1665 and volume ix is dated 1664 or is undated. The Dutch edition frequently appears together with the two town atlases of the Netherlands in a uniform style of binding.

Famous copies of the Dutch edition are preserved in the University Library of Amsterdam, in an original 17th-century cabinet in which the volumes were displayed as show pieces; in the Maritime Museum in Amsterdam, de luxe Magnus bindings with the coats of arms of Jan van Loon and Wendela Bas; in the Atlas van Stolk in Rotterdam, de luxe bindings with the arms of the Van Bergen van der Grijp family.

Locations: Sixteen copies in Holland. Only a few copies outside Holland, i.a. Library of Congress; British Museum; Bibliothèque Nationale, Paris; University Library, Ghent; Public Library, Warsaw.

The edition with German text

It is doubtful whether the German major atlas was ever offered for sale as such. The nine volumes all bear a pasted-on title *Atlas Major Dasz ist Weltbeschreibung*, but the copies are actually no more than compilations of the *Theatrum*. The catalogue of 1670 does not list a German edition. It seems probable that the German *Atlas Maior* was compiled to order.

Two copies are known: University Library, Göttingen and Staatliche Bibliothek, Bamberg.

The edition with Spanish text

The Spanish edition is the rarest of all the editions even though Blaeu had started printing it before the others. It was never completed, however, since the material for volume xi was destroyed by the fire of 1672. A quantity of the printed sheets was possibly also burnt, which may account for the rarity of the edition.

After the fire, ten-volume copies of the Spanish edition were compiled from the sheets with Spanish text which could not, however, be backed by maps, since the plates had melted in the fire. In Blaeu's printing office these sheets with Spanish texts were pasted on the reverse (letterpress side) of sheets printed in French, Latin, or Dutch. Copies of the *Atlas Mayor* made up in this way are considered as belonging to the second edition.

Shortly after the fire, the Amsterdam book collector Goswinus Uilenbroek procured eight damaged unbound copies of the Spanish edition from which he compiled one complete copy. This fact is recorded in the sales catalogue of Uilenbroek's book collection.[20]

Turkish transcriptions[21]

In 1685 or thereabouts Joan Blaeu's *Atlas Maior* was translated and copied by Ebu Bakir, a son of Behran ed Dimenski. This manuscript atlas which is preserved in the library of the Topkapi Serail Museum in Istanbul comprises nine volumes measuring 34 × 22 cm. Of the nearly 600 maps, 246 have been accurately copied and supplied with Turkish names. Even the decorative elements have been faithfully reproduced in details such as the ships which are shown flying the Dutch colours. The copyist went to work selectively, reducing the number of maps of England and France, but adopting practically all the maps of Asia and America. It should be mentioned for the sake of the record that both the *Atlas* and the *Atlas Minor* of Mercator-Hondius were likewise transcribed into Turkish.

A Monsieur

Colbert

Conseiller du Roy

en son Conseil Roijal

des Finances

et Intendant des

Finances.

que l'amour que sa Majesté a pour toutes les belles choses, luy inspire; et j'ay espoir de ce que la
renommée récente de vostre modestie & de vostre affabilité, que vous ne me refuserez pas la grace que je vous
demande, qui est d'offrir au Roy l'hommage que ie luy rends, comme au plus Grand, au plus Genereux,
& au plus Sage Monarque du Monde. Si mon Livre a l'honneur d'estre placé dans son Cabinet, si sa
Majesté y daigne ietter les yeux en passant; & si mon travail ne luy desplaist pas, mon ambition
sera entierement satisfaite; car je suis asseuré que le jugement favorable du meilleur & du plus esclairé
Prince qui ait jamais esté, sera capable de faire la bonne fortune de mon Ouvrage, & d'en establir la
reputation. Je suis

Monsieur

Vostre treshumble & tres obeissant Serviteur

J. Blaeu.

D'Amsterdam le 1 Janvier 1664.

15. First and last part of Joan Blaeu's dedication to Colbert, written by hand in the
copy of the *Grand Atlas* preserved by the Amsterdam University Library.

5. The cartographical contents of the Grand Atlas

VOLUME I

Northern Europe, Norway, Denmark, and Schleswig

The first volume' of the *Grand Atlas* opens with a dedication by Joan Blaeu to Louis XIV dated 1 January 1663. Below this is Blaeu's autograph dedication to the French minister of finance Colbert. This is therefore a unique presentation copy to the minister. At some time or other, this copy must have passed into the trade and in 1962 it was acquired by the University Library of Amsterdam. The other editions of the *Atlas Maior* contain printed dedications to other heads of state, the Dutch edition being dedicated to the States-General of the United Republic, the Latin to the emperor Leopold II, and the Spanish to King Philip IV.

Preface and introduction are followed by a typographical title-page which precedes the impressive allegorical representation with the title *Geographia Blaviana*. The crowned figure of Science, holding a key, is depicted on a triumphal chariot, accompanied by the symbolical figures of Europe, Asia, Africa, and America.

An introduction to cosmography,i.e. a treatise on the mathematical description of the features of the heavens and the earth, is presented in the first fourteen pages of text.

The first map is a map of the world in two hemispheres in stereographic projection that was specially designed for the *Atlas Maior* as a new map of the world. During the three previous

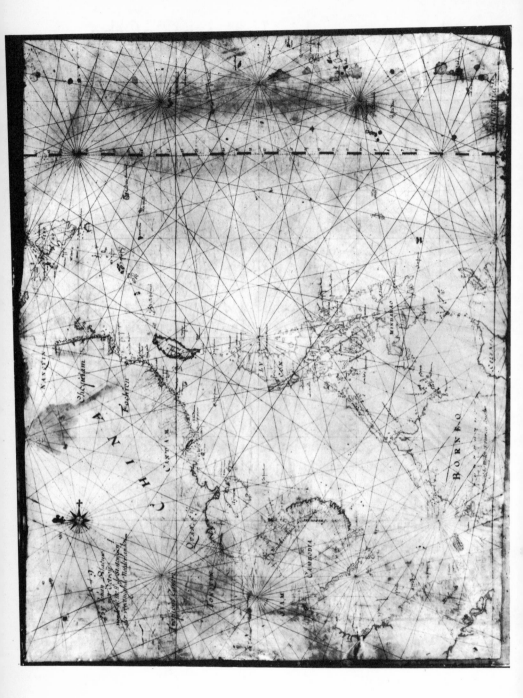

17. Printed chart on vellum published by Pieter and Joan Blaeu II in 1677.

18. The 'Latin School' in Gravenstraat where the second printing house of the Blaeus was situated in 1667; destroyed by fire in 1672. Detail from the plan of Amsterdam by Balthasar Florisz. van Berckenrode, 1647.

18a. One of the decorative 'tail pieces' in the *Grand Atlas*.

decades, Blaeu had used the world map in Mercator's Projection, with the seven wonders of the world in the border ornamentation (Nova tertius terrarum orbis geographica tabula).

The second map, of the Arctic, had been made in 1638 for the *Theatrum*, the dedication being added in 1642.

Maps (3)-(8), showing the islands in the Arctic Ocean, were also made specially for the *Atlas Maior*. Maps (9) and (10), on the other hand, derive from the *Atlantis Appendix* of 1630.

The part devoted to Europe is introduced by a symbolical figure of Europe followed by a typographical title-piece. These individual title-pieces appear throughout the atlas. In the Latin edition, moreover, the various parts are preceded by dedications to the sovereigns of the respective countries. The Norwegian maps (11)-(17) are new with the exception of map (12) 'Diocesis Stavangriensis' which dates from 1638. After Norway comes Denmark, with the majority of the maps specially engraved for the *Atlas Maior*, except maps (18) and (22) which also date from 1638. This is followed by an extremely interesting section showing illustrations of astronomical instruments.

The plates illustrating the instruments from Tycho Brahe's observatory

With the aid of a grant from King Frederick II of Denmark, the famous astronomer Tycho Brahe built an observatory which he called Uranienborg on the Isle of Hven in 1576. Willem Blaeu was one of the many foreigners who came to study at Hven. An entry in Tycho Brahe's diary of 27 May 1596 records:' Abijt domum in Hollandium Wilhelmus Batavius cum per integram hyemem hic fuisset'.[22] Tycho Brahe also mentions in a letter to Tobias Fischer that Blaeu had spent six months with him. This does not tally with Joan Blaeu's statement in the *Atlas Maior* that his father had spent two whole years at Tycho Brahe's. Despite the ambiguity concerning the length of his stay, we definitely know, by the testimony of the astronomer himself among others, that Willem Blaeu had studied astronomy and cosmography under Tycho Brahe, that he had carried out observations and constructed celestial globes and astronomical instruments.

Willem Blaeu also constructed a map of the Isle of Hven 'Insula Hvaena sive Venusia, à Guiljelmo Blaeu, cum sub Tychone astronomiae operam daret, delineatea', which was, however, first incorporated in the atlas by his son Joan in the *Atlas Maior* (map (25) in the *Grand Atlas*).[23]

The eleven plates with illustrations of Uranienborg and the instruments, which were included in the first volume of the *Atlas Maior* by Joan Blaeu, were probably never issued by Willem Blaeu himself. They are revised copies of the woodcuts appearing in *Tychones Brahe Astronomiae instauratiae mechanicae* ... 1598, from which work the descriptive text likewise derives. These plates rightly belong in the Danish section which also includes the new map 'Scania'.

In the first volume of the *Grand Atlas* Joan Blaeu incorporated a large number of up-to-date maps that were absolutely first-rate, thereby compensating for the rather dated contents of the atlas as a whole. These were the maps of Schleswig and Holstein made by Iohannes Mejer. From 1638 to 1648 Iohannes Mejer (1606-1674), Royal Mathematician to King Christian IV, later to King Frederick III, and a pupil of Tycho Brahe's, had mapped the territory of Schleswig and Holstein with astonishing accuracy. The project was executed under the aegis of the Duke of Schleswig-Holstein, Frederick IV. Of but few other regions in Europe at the time did so detailed a map exist. Most of the original surveys have been lost, but the map formed the base for forty general maps which were engraved in copper by Matthias and Nicolaus Petersen, goldsmiths of Husum, and the engravers A. and Chr. Lorensen. These maps were engraved for Casparus

Danckwerth's book, *Newe Landesbeschreibung der zweij Herzog-thümer Schleswig und Holstein*, published in 1652. The book had no success, however, partly as a result of ducal disapprobation. Two brothers of the author, the chamberlain Joachim Danckwerth of Schleswig and the apothecary Samuel Danckwerth of Copen-hagen, had helped to finance the venture. After the death of Casparus Danckwerth, litigation ensued between Iohannes Mejer and the heirs. It was at this time that the copper-plates were sold by Danckwerth's widow to Joan Blaeu for the ridiculously low price of 360 Thaler. Adam Olearius, court mathematician at Gottorp acted as intermediary in the transaction. Joan Blaeu in-cluded 34 of the 40 maps in Danckwerth's 'Description' in his *Grand Atlas*, 21 in volume I and 13 in volume III, the latter being maps of Holstein which for geo-political reasons Blaeu considered expedient to incorporate with Germany (volume III). No addi-tions or alterations were made in the plates. Since Blaeu did not even add his own imprint, the difference from the maps in Danckwerth's book is barely perceptible, witness the facsimile edition *Die Landkarten von Johannes Mejer . . . mit einer Einleitung von Dr. Christian Degn*, published by Otto Heinevetter, Hamburg-Bergedorf, 1963.

VOLUME II
Sweden, Russia, Poland, Eastern Europe, and Greece

The second volume contains three-sevenths of what Blaeu called the atlas of Europe. It opens with the maps of Sweden.

Sweden
   Maps (1), (2), (3), (5), (6), and (8) were engraved after the

original manuscript maps of the Swedish surveyor Andreas Bureus. Though the remaining Swedish maps (4), (7), (9), and (10) are not credited to Bureus, they may possibly have been engraved after his originals. The first map in volume II, also by Bureus, had appeared in the *Theatrum* in 1635. Maps (4), (7), (8), and (10) date from 1638. The other maps of Sweden were first issued in the *Atlas Maior*.

Andreas Bureus was the head of the Swedish Land Survey, founded in 1628.[24] He was already known for his map of Lapland, drawn in 1611, and for his map of the northern regions, 'Orbis arctoi', in 1626. Bureus surveyed and drew other maps of the Swedish provinces after 1628, of which the originals have not been traced until now. According to Swedish authors[25], Willem Blaeu was granted the privilege to publish them. Friberg assumes that the Blaeu maps were based on Bureus's 'Orbis arctoi' and that Bureus's map of Dalecarlia was used by Blaeu's rival Johannes Janssonius. But since Friberg could not consult the other original provincial maps by Bureus, their contents may well have agreed with the maps of Sweden published in the *Atlas Maior*.

Russia

The origin of the general map of Russia is noteworthy. It was designed in 1613 by Hessel Gerritsz. This date appears on the first state of the engraving. The second state bears the date 1614 and the imprint of Hessel Gerritsz. In 1635 the map was included in the *Theatrum* with the imprint 'Amstelodami, Excusum apud Guiljelmum Blaeu'. When the *Grand Atlas* was being produced, the plate was therefore fifty years old. This part further contains three maps representing South, West, North and East Russia respectively, viz. maps (12), (15), and (16). The first- and last-mentioned had appeared in Blaeu's *Theatrum* in 1638. Map (15),

'Russiae, vulgo Moscovia dictae, Pars Occidentalis', is from the hand of Isaac Massa. Though first included in an atlas in the *Atlas Maior* in 1662, it originated around 1610 and is based on Isaac Massa's itinerary *Beschrijvinghe van der Samoyeden Landt in Tartarien*. Map (17) in this section, and presumably also map (18), is by the Holstein scholar Adam Olearius (1599-1671) whose name has cropped up in connexion with the plates of the Schleswig and Holstein maps which Blaeu acquired from Danckwerth. Olearius was the author of the giant Gottorp globe constructed in 1664. This fact also points to contact with Joan Blaeu. Both these maps (17) and (18) were first issued in 1662.

The Town Plans of Moscow

The town plans (13) and (14), though not previously included in an atlas, ante-date 1630. This has been established by their inclusion in a copy of Willem Blaeu's *Atlantis Appendix* of 1630 in the library of the Major Seminary Liesbosch-Prinsenhage at Breda.[26] Both maps, with plain backs, were added to the atlas together with a number of other maps dating from the period 1620-1630. The plans of Moscow and the Kremlin were doubtless engraved after Russian originals, and the presumption seems justified that they derived from Hessel Gerritsz who is known to have had Russian maps in his possession, on which he based his map 'Tabula Russiae ex autographo, quod delineandum curavit Foedor filius Azaris Boris desumta . . . 1613'. It is possible that the town plans likewise derived from the above-mentioned Fyodor, son of Czar Boris Godunov (1598-1605). There is a similarity between the inset on the map of Hessel Gerritsz and the town plan. Three states are known of the 'Tabula Russiae'. The third state, with text and the imprint of Willem Blaeu, was first included in the atlas of 1635.

Poland

Seven of the ten maps devoted to Poland were first issued in the *Atlas Maior* in 1662, only three of them, (19), (22), and (24), ante-dating 1638. Joan Blaeu credits map (20) to G. Frueden-kamer and map (23) to Olaf Iohannes Gotho. The identity of the authors of the remaining maps is not known, but Blaeu does mention that the texts of the descriptive accounts derived from Salomon Neugebauer and Simon Strovolsci.[27] A remarkable map is shown of the river Dnepr which is depicted in eight sections on four plates (25)-(28). The author of the original survey is most probably Beauplan.

Eastern Europe

Maps (29)-(32) and map (34) derive from the first *Theatrum* edition of 1635. Map (33), 'Illyricum Hodiernum', with a dedication by Blaeu to Petrus de Zrin, is here issued for the first time. It was not included in the 1662 Latin edition, nor is it listed yet in the index of the *Grand Atlas*.

Greece

There are no up-to-date maps in this part. Maps (35)-(38) date from 1640. Though the remaining maps in volume II, (39) and (40), were first issued by Blaeu in his *Atlas Maior* in 1662, they were not original. These maps of the Greek archipelago, by the hand of Joannes Laurenbergius, were copied from the maps issued in 1650 by Johannes Janssonius in his *Atlas Maritimus*.

VOLUME III
Germany

This volume contains 97 maps, more than any of the other volumes. It is not easy to trace the provenance of all these maps, since there is no German carto-bibliography such as exists of the maps of Scotland.

We can distinguish in the first instance between existing copperplates and those engraved specially for the *Atlas Maior*. No less than 42 maps were first issued in atlas form in the *Atlas Maior*, but 13 of these were printed from the copper-plates which Joan Blaeu had acquired from Dankwerth's *Newe Landesbeschreibung der zwey Herzogthümer Schleswig und Holstein* (cf. the discussion of these maps in the analysis of volume 1), viz. maps (41)-(50), (52) -(54). The remaining 29 new maps are (1), (3), (7)-(9), (11), (12), (14), (15), (19), (23)-(25), (28), (29), (33)-(36), (39), (55), (59), (74), (78), (84), (85), (87), (89), (94), (95). Most of the maps of Germany, however, were issued before 1650. These can be classified as follows:

first issued in 1649, in *Toonneel des Aerdrijcks*: (32), (58)
first issued in 1642, in *Toonneel des Aerdrijcks*: (6)
first issued in (1635-1638?), in *l'Appendice*: (10), (13), (30), (57), (61), (75), (80), (86)
first issued in or before 1635: all the remaining maps.

Map (84) 'Franconia vulgo Franckenlandt' deserves special mention. This map did not appear in the Latin edition but was first included in the French edition of the *Atlas Maior*.

The regional maps of Germany were a constant source of interest to Joan Blaeu. In 1638, shortly after its completion, he added 8 maps of German *Länder* to the two-volume *Novus Atlas*, among them the maps of Silesia, Glatz, and Lausnitz which were derived from the original maps of Jonas Scultetus Sprottau (=

Johann Schultz of Sprottau, 1603-1664).[28] Among the 42 new maps of 1662 we also find maps of Silesia by Johann Schultz, viz. maps (11), (12), (13), and (15) which presumably date from 1650 or thereabouts. There are at least thirteen unsigned maps among the later additions of 1662. They should probably be regarded as compilations by Joan Blaeu himself. Other regional maps of Germany are credited to:

(8) Frederick Kuhnovio Bolcos (not in Bonacker)
(23) Nicolaus Ritterhausen aus Altorf (1597-1670)
(26), (35), (36) Olaf Joh. Gotho (= Olof Hansson Örnehufvud, a Swedish surveyor from Brandenburg, c.1640)
(94) Johann Rauw, cosmographer († 1600)

VOLUME IV
The Netherlands

This volume consists of two parts, the Southern Netherlands (*Pays Bas*) and the United Republic (*Belgique Confederée*), comprising 63 maps all told. The first part contains 17 and the second part 13 maps not printed before by Blaeu. The early editions of Blaeu's *Theatrum*, 1642-1658, contained 35 maps of the Netherlands. This means that the number of maps was almost doubled, whereas two old plates were discarded, which is a considerably greater expansion than in any of the other volumes. The volume of the Netherlands affords a striking example of Joan Blaeu's opportunist methods. Nearly all his additions were printed from old, often very old plates. It is amazing to find Blaeu putting up with such outdated material where his own country was concerned. It is no less amazing that he retained almost all the antiquated maps from his atlases of 1630-1635.

The volume opens with the well-known map of the XVII

Provinces which had been issued by Willem Blaeu in 1608. The first issue had a decorative border and a cartouche surrounding the privilege dated '26 Martij 1608'. The border ornamentation, cartouche and privilege were omitted in the second state which was included in the *Atlantis Appendix* of 1630, but it was only in 1642 that the name 'Guliel. Janssonio' was superseded by 'Guliel. Blaeu' in the imprint. A few other maps go back to the early years of Willem Blaeu:

(6) Tabula Castelli ad Sandflitam. First included in the *Atlantis Appendix*, 1630.

(41) Tractus Rheni et Mosae. First included in the *Atlantis Appendix*, 1630.

(57) Ultraiectum Dominium. This plate was procured by Willem Blaeu from Jodocus Hondius II in 1629 and the name of Hondius was superseded by that of Willem Blaeu.

(58) Frisia Occidentalis. Also acquired from Jodocus Hondius. Copied from the original by the Franeker professor Adriaan Metius, issued in 1622.[29]

(60) Groninga Dominium. Also acquired from Jodocus Hondius. Copied from the original by the Groningen patrician Barthold Wickeringe, issued in 1616.

(63) Tabula Bargarum ad Zomam. Constructed by the Leiden professor Frans van Schooten in 1622 during the siege of the town by Prince Maurice.

The following maps which also go back to the time of Willem Blaeu were first included in the *Appendix*, 1631:

(2) Brabantia Ducatus

(18) Pars Flandria Teutonica occidentalior

(35) Archiepiscopatus Cameracensis

(37) Geldria ducatus et Zutfania comitatus

(43) Zuydhollandia stricte sumta

(44) Delflandia, Schielandia, et insula trans Mosam

(45) Rhenolandiae et Amstellandiae exactissima Tabula
(46) Hollandia Pars Septentrionalis
The maps (18) and (46) mentioned above are noteworthy for being among the first on which the name of Joan Blaeu appears in a joint imprint. The maps of North and South Holland, dating from 1630 or thereabouts, were copied by Willem Blaeu from the existing maps in the Mercator-Hondius atlas. These Hondius maps were based on the large-scale map of Holland made by Balthasar Florisz van Berckenrode between 1620 and 1621.

The following fifteen regional maps of the Netherlands were introduced in the first edition of Willem Blaeu's *Theatrum* in 1635:
(3) Prima Pars Brabantiae
(4) Secunda Pars Brabantiae
(5) Tertia Pars Brabantiae

These three sheets were based on the large-scale survey of Brabant by Michael Florisz van Langren who played an important role in Dutch cartography. He constructed several topographical campaign maps in the period 1620-1630, and until about 1740 his maps of Brabant were the best that were available of that region.[30]

(7) Ducatus Limburgum. Copied from an early map by Aegidius Martini dating from 1603 which appeared in the Mercator-Hondius Atlas, 1611.

(8) Lutzenburg Ducatus. A new title added to the plate from 1635 that had been copied from a map in the Mercator-Hondius Atlas.

(9) Flandria et Zeelandia Comitatus.

(22) Flandriae Partus duae.

(28) Galloflandria. Copied from the original by the French cartographer Martin Doué (1572-1638).[31]

(29) Artesia Comitatus.

(30) Comitatuum Harmoniae.

(31) Namurcum Comitatus. Copied from a very early map by Joh. Surhon, which had already appeared in the *Theatrum* of Abraham Ortelius in 1570.

(32) Mechlinia Dominium. Likewise by the well-known cartographer Michael Florisz van Langren, about 1630.

(42) Hollandia Comitatus. In 1635 this map superseded Willem Blaeu's early map with the emblazoned coats of arms, which had itself been copied from Willem Blaeu's spectacular map of Holland with costumed figures and views (first issue 1604 regarded as Willem Blaeu's first map).

(55) Zeelandia Comitatus.

(62) Quarta Pars Brabantiae. Made by Willebrord van der Burght. This map had appeared in the atlas of Hondius in 1633. The map of Willem Blaeu is known in proof state without coats of arms in the margins.

Prior to the inclusion of thirty 'new' maps of the Netherlands in Joan Blaeu's atlas in 1662, the publisher had introduced only one innovation in the entire period 1625-1662:

(61) Drentia Comitatus which was included in Blaeu's *Appendice* of 1638. It is a reduced version of a map issued in 1634 by Cornelis Pynacker.[32]

Then the following thirty 'new' maps were issued in 1662: (10-17), (19-21), (23)-(27), (33), (36), (38)-(40), (47)-(52), (54)-(56). It should be observed that most of this material, unfortunately, was anything but fresh. We find, for instance, the following maps from the *Flandria Illustrata* of Sanderus dating from 1641: (10)-(17), (19)-(21), (23)-(27). Also the maps of the four quarters of Gelderland copied from the originals by Nicolaas Geelkercken in the book of J. I. Pontanus of 1639: nos. (33), (38)-(40). Though included for the first time in a Blaeu atlas, the following Dutch polder maps could harldy have passed as up-to-date in 1662:

(47) Agri Zypani Nova Descript. Printed from a considerably revised plate by Pieter van der Keere, 1617.

(48) Agri Biemstrani. Also printed from an original plate by Pieter van der Keere, 1617.

(49) Caerte van de Scher-meer. An anonymous map issued short-ly after 1635.

(50) Kaerte van de Buyckslooter . . . Meeren. An early map by C. J. Visscher, first issued c. 1630.

(51) Kaerte van alle de Sanden, Gorsingen, Slicken, Waerden end Kreecken . . . genoemt het Koe-gras. A map by C. J. Visscher, c. 1620.

(52) Territorii Bergensis Accuratissima Descriptio. This fine map by the surveyor Johannes Dou dates from c. 1640.

The only regional maps of the United Republic with a legitimate claim to the qualification 'new' are the four following:

(54) Walachria.

(55) Utraque Bevelandia.

(56) Zelandiae Pars Transscaldina.

(59) Transisaliania Provincia; vulgo Over-Yssel. Copied from Nic. ten Have's large-scale map of Overijssel, 1652.

VOLUME V
England

There is no difficulty in establishing the provenance of the maps in this volume of the *Grand Atlas*. Comparison with John Speed's *Theatre of the Empire of Great Britaine* (first edition, 1611-12) reveals that Joan Blaeu had the main part of his maps engraved after those of Speed. And comparison with Camden's *Britannia* (first edition with maps, 1607) makes it clear that Joan Blaeu derived the text of his atlas from him. This is the easier understood because an issue of this work had been printed by Willem Blaeu in 1617 and a miniature edition in pocket size was published by him in 1639.

Blaeu utilized maps from various editons of Speed's *Theatre*. According to Skelton[33], the 59 maps in Volume v of the *Grand Atlas* derive from the following sources:

5 maps from Speed, pre-1623 state.
41 maps from Speed, post-1623 state.
7 maps from Speed, of uncertain date
6 maps from Hondius-Mercator atlas.

Skelton's analysis was based on the first issue of Blaeu's atlas of England, 1645. This should have no effect, however, on the evaluation of the 1663 edition, since there were no alterations in the plates between 1645 and 1667 (last printing) as far as we know. (With the exception of the maps of Cornwall, Sussex, and Leicester to which small compass roses were added in 1649). Before Blaeu issued his atlas of England in 1645, he had included two English maps in his *Theatrum*, viz. (1) and (3) together with the maps 'Scotia Regnum' and 'Hibernia Regnum'. These four maps appeared in a small supplement that was inserted at the back of volume III of the *Theatrum*, 1640 (cf. Koeman, *Atlantes Neerlandici*, I, p. 35 C, p. 36 B, p. 38 B, p. 41 A).

The geographical content of these maps was derived from Speed but there can be no doubt that Blaeu put his own characteristic stamp on them by the addition of ornaments and coats of arms. His imprint only appeared on four maps, however.

Here (and in the atlas of Scotland as we shall see later) we find maps that were thirty years old or more at the time of issue. But in the 17th century this was a matter of minor importance.

Blaeu also derived his title-page illustrations from Speed. The frontispiece shows the figures of 'Normannus' and 'Danus' standing in recesses. On the upper panel 'Britannicus' is flanked by

'Saxo' and 'Romanus'. Above these panels are the bearings of England with the lion and unicorn (minus horn!). From 1645 onwards this title-page featured in all editions.

A new privilege, dated 1 January 1662, was granted for the *Grand Atlas*. The date on the frontispiece is 1663 or 1662. The existence of variants dated 1662 of the French edition of the *Grand Atlas*, which is usually dated 1663, was discovered by Skelton (op. cit. p. 117). The rivalry between Blaeu and Janssonius is clearly demonstrated in their atlases of England. After the issue of Blaeu's atlas in 1645, Janssonius followed with his in 1646, despite the fact that he had previously included 29 county maps in his atlases.

VOLUME VI
Scotland and Ireland

The volume containing the maps of Scotland is the best authenticated by contemporary records. Compared with our ignorance of the sources utilized by Joan Blaeu in his maps of countries such as Poland and Germany, we are amply informed on the provenance of the maps of Scotland. These maps were engraved after manuscript originals by Timothy Pont, a minister, from his survey of a large part of Scotland from 1596 to about 1600, augmented with information supplied by Robert Gordon and prepared for the press by the latter. Robert Gordon, who was a skilled cartographer, also wrote a dedication for Blaeu's atlas of Scotland. It is evident, therefore, that the material on which this atlas was based was more than fifty years old at the time of publication. Yet the Amsterdam cartographers must have known about Timothy Pont's surveys by 1610, since one of the many maps engraved by Jodocus Hondius II († 1612) is entitled 'A new Description of the Shyres Lothian and Linlitquo Be T. Pont' and bears the imprint 'Jodocus Hondius caelavit sumptibus Andreae Hart'. Andrew Hart was an Edinburgh bookseller who had only this one map of Pont's engraved in Amsterdam. It was not till 1630, however, that this map was first included in the French edition of the Mercator-Hondius atlas.

Documentary evidence concerning the cartographic reproduction of Pont's manuscript surveys is provided in several surviving letters of King Charles I, Robert Gordon, Sir John Scot, Willem and Joan Blaeu, and others. A detailed reconstruction of the history is given in R. A. Skelton's article 'County Atlases of the British Isles', part 3.[34]

The documents show, as Skelton points out, that the manuscript sketches of the survey of Scotland passed into the possession of Sir James Balfour of Kinnaird (1600-1657). Balfour did not succeed in having the maps engraved and delegated the matter to Sir John Scot(t) of Scotstarvet (1585-1670). From the surviving correspondence between Sir John Scot and the Blaeus (16 letters in the National Library of Scotland, Edinburgh) we know that Scot sent the first maps to Willem Blaeu to be engraved in 1631 or thereabouts. Progress was rather slow, however, and the old manuscripts cannot have been very satisfactory. In 1641 Willem Blaeu's son Joan took up the matter again, sending several proof sheets to Scot who showed them to King Charles I (cf. Skelton, op. cit. p. 101). As a result, Robert Gordon was authorized by the King on 8 October 1641 to amend and supplement the proof states. On 10 March 1642 Joan Blaeu wrote to Scot about supplementary material for Pont's maps. Titles, coats of arms, town views, etc. were lacking and there were no maps at all of the north of Scotland. Robert Gordon constructed the maps of the missing regions. These were 'Scotiae provinciae mediterraneae inter Taum flumen et Vararis aestuarium' and 'Estima Scotiae

Septentrionalis ara'. In 1645 Sir John Scot himself came to Amsterdam to look over the maps with Blaeu and particularly to check and supplement the descriptive text. But it was not till 1649 that Blaeu informed Scot that printing had started on the atlas and that he hoped to complete it in the same year if the missing texts were delivered in time. Because of various political troubles, this material for which Robert Gordon was responsible did not reach Blaeu till 1653. Only one of these maps, however, 'Scotia Antiqua', is actually dated 1653. The other maps are undated, which is understandable considering the old geographical material on which they were based. A privilege was granted by the States-General on 18 June 1654 and the imprints of the first issue of the Latin, French, German, and Dutch editions are all dated 1654. The imprint of the first Spanish edition also bears the date 1654, though the privilege is dated 24 March 1659. Several versions and editions of the atlas of Scotland sew the light between 1654 and 1667. There were no alterations, however, in the number of the maps nor in the contents, except for the compass roses added to the plates of 28 maps after 1665 (cf. Skelton op. cit. p. 121).

The atlas comprised 55 maps all told, 48 maps of Scotland, 6 of Ireland, and one historical map of the British Isles. The maps of Scotland were not all based on the surveys of Timothy Pont. The following maps should all (or presumably all) be attributed to Robert Gordon: (2), (13), (30)-(34), (36)-(38), and (48).

Map (8) had been engraved by Jodocus Hondius after an original by Pont before 1612. Blaeu's map is a copy of this map in the atlas of Janssonius. Map (49) 'Orcadum et Schetlandiae Insularum' was engraved after an original by Pont which, on the evidence of a letter from Willem Blaeu to Sir John Scot, was in Blaeu's possession by August 1626. This map was included in

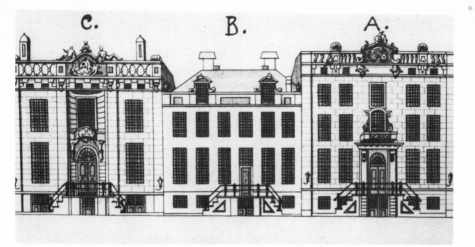

19. The house on 541 Herengracht where Joan Blaeu II lived from 1696 to 1712. From Caspar Philipsz.' 'Grachtenboek' of Amsterdam.

20a. One of the many coats of arms decorating the maps in the *Grand Atlas*.

20. The book-case designed for the 12-volume facsimile edition of Joan Blaeu's *Grand Atlas*.

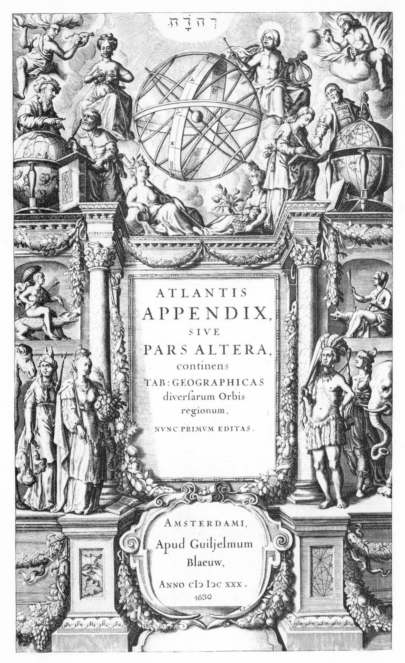

21. Frontispiece of Willem Jansz. Blaeu's first atlas, the *Atlantis Appendix*, 1630.

CIVITATES
STATVS ECCLESIASTICI

22. Allegorical title page of the *Citta del Vaticano* volume of Joan Blaeu's Townbooks of Italy, published in 1663.

Blaeu's early atlases. In his turn, Henricus Hondius copied this map of the Orkney Islands in 1636 for his Mercator atlas.

The six maps of Ireland were all copied from maps in the atlas of Janssonius, and he had copied them from maps in Speed's *Theatre of Great Britaine*. Janssonius did not, however, follow the example set by Blaeu in publishing an atlas of Scotland as he had done with his atlas of England which was issued in 1646.

The bibliographical history of the atlas of Scotland after 1654 is particularly fascinating, as it is interwoven with the political history of England and Holland. Skelton (op. cit. pp. 103-105) gives a clear exposition in his bibliography of the variants which occurred in the preliminary matter of the atlas – dedications, privileges, etc. – in the period 1654-1662. Joan Blaeu's dedication to the Royalist Sir John Scot, for example, was omitted in the copies sold in England. The text of the 1662 *Grand Atlas* under discussion here was reprinted from the 1654 edition and here too the dedication to Sir John Scot is missing, though Robert Gordon's letter to Scot is included.

It may be of interest to draw attention to the fact noted by Skelton in his bibliography[35] (p. 104) that Sir John Scot's presentation copy of the 1665 Blaeu atlas is preserved in the Library of Congress (Phillips 5941). The presentation copy of Robert Gordon has also survived. It is in Aberdeen University Library.

VOLUMES VII AND VIII
France and Switzerland

Volume VII comprises 37 maps, and volume VIII 30 maps of France (plus 6 maps of Switzerland). For this reason both these volumes are discussed here in one chapter. There could only have been one plausible argument for spreading the 67 maps of France over two volumes, namely that the number of volumes in the *Grand Atlas* should exceed those of the other editions of the *Atlas Maior*. This was probably a question of sales policy, for seventy-three maps will fit comfortably into one not over large binding.

The *Grand Atlas* contains 67 regional maps of France, against 64 in the Latin edition and 66 in the Dutch. The three maps which are not included in the Latin edition are: (1) Gallia Vetus; (2) Typus veteris; (15) Archiepiscopatus Cameracensis (new version).

If we analyse the contents of Volumes VII and VIII, we find that here too Blaeu went to work with a certain opportunism. Retaining the greater part of the maps issued by his father in 1631 and 1635, he added only 22 new maps to the *Grand Atlas*. The 67 maps of France in volumes VII and VIII can be classified as follows:

a) deriving from the *Atlantis Appendix*, 1630: map (14) in vol. VIII;

b) deriving from the *Appendix*, 1631: 24 maps.
   In vol. VII: (6), (9), (12), (15), (17), (18), (23) halfsheet, (26), (29) halfsheet, (30), (32), (36), (37).
   In vol. VIII: (1), (5), (7) halfsheet, (10) halfsheet, (11), (13), (15), (25)-(27), (29).

c) deriving from the *Theatrum*, 1635: 19 maps.
   In vol. VII: (1), (2), (4), (5), (10), (11), (13), (20), (24), (27), (28), (33), (35).
   In vol. VIII: (4), (16), (18), (19), (22) not in index, (28).

d) deriving from the *Theatrum*, 1650: map (16) in vol. VII, Nova Picardiae Tabula.

e) 22 new maps added 1662-1664.
   In vol. VII: (3), (7), (8), (14), (19), (21) not in index, (22), (25), (31), (34).
   In vol. VIII: (2), (3), (6), (8), (9), (12) not in index, (17), (20), (21), (23), (24), (30) not in index.

The inclusion of a large number of maps of the provinces of France would obviously have benefited the sales of the French editions of Blaeu's atlases. In this respect, also, Willem Blaeu emulated the Mercator-Hondius atlas which had already included 12 maps of France in 1619. In 1631 Johannes Janssonius issued his *Theatrum Universae Galliae*[36], containing 50 maps of France, nearly all of them copied from M. Bouguereau and J. le Clerc (see below) and signed by Henricus and/or Jodocus Hondius. With this publication, Janssonius surpassed Willem Blaeu's 1631 *Appendix* in which 29 maps of France had been included. Janssonius was to maintain the lead in this field until Joan Blaue issued the *Atlas Maior* in 1662.

We have no difficulty in establishing the provenance of the maps in volumes VII and VIII. Excellent French atlases with maps of the provinces existed even before 1630: B. Bouguereau's *Le Théatre Francoys*, first issue 1594[37], and Jean le Clerc's *Le Théatre géographique du Royaume de France*, first issue 1619.[38] Willem Blaeu either had his maps of France engraved after these originals or in some instances copied from the maps of Hondius.

It is remarkable that signatures mainly appear on the French maps which Willem Blaeu had had engraved for his *Appendix*, 1631 and his *Theatrum*. The majority of these signed maps are listed below with mention of the author's name and first date of issue. We are indebted for this information to the article by F. de Dainville on J. le Clerc's *Théatre géograhique du Royaume de France*.

In volume VII:
(4) Le Gouvernement de L'Isle de France. Copied from a map by Damien de Templeux, issued by J. le Clerc, in 1617.
(5) Ager Parisiensis vulgo L'Isle de France. Copied from a map by Fr. de la Guillotiére, issued by J. le Clerc in 1619.

(12) Dioecese de Rhenis, et le païs de Rethel. Copied from a map by J. Jubrien, issued by J. le Clerc in 1621.

(17) Descriptio Veromanduorum. After an early map by Joh. Surhon, issued by M. Bouguereau in 1592.

(26) Ducatus Andegavensis. After an early map by Licino Guyeto, first issued by M. Bouguereau in 1591.

(29) Comitatus Blesensis. Copied from a map by J. du Temps (= Johannes Temporius), issued by J. le Clerc in 1619.

(30) Ducatus Turonensis. After an early map by Isaac Franco, first issued by M. Bouguereau in 1592.

(36) a. Lemovicum; b. Topographia Limaniae. After an early map by Joh. Fayano, issued by M. Bouguereau in 1594.

In volume VIII:

(4) Dioecesis Sarlatensis. Copied from a map by Joannus Tarde, issued by J. le Clerc in 1626.

(13) Provincia. Copied from a map by P. J. Bompart (= Bomparius), issued by J. le Clerc in 1619.

(15) Delphinatus vulgo Dauphiné. Copied from a map by Jean de Beins, issued by J. le Clerc in 1622.

(25) Territorium Metense. After a map by Ab. Fabert, issued by J. le Clerc in 1617.

(28) Lacus Lemanni. After a map by S. Goulart, issued by J. le Clerc in 1619.

Of the 22 maps which were added to the *Grand Atlas* in the period 1662-1664, only two are signed, viz. maps (8) and (10) in volume VIII, both by the Royal Cartographer Pierre du Val (1618-1683).

The remaining maps of France published by Blaeu in the period 1630-1635 most probably also derived from maps originally issued by Le Clerc. We know, for instance, 7 maps signed by Damien de Templeux and 5 more attributed to him, all of them made for Jean le Clerc.[39] Among Blaeu's provincial maps of

France we find many unsigned specimens which could have been copied from De Templeux.

This analysis leads to the conclusion that in 1663 the *Grand Atlas* included no fewer than 43 maps of the provinces of France ante-dating 1620 (4 of which ante-date 1595!), all of them based on maps previously issued in atlas form, and that this lack of up-to-date geographical information was only counterbalanced to a limited extent by the 22 new additions.

Switzerland

Volume VIII contains 6 maps of Switzerland, the first 4 of which were copied from maps in the atlas of Gerard Mercator, *Galliae Tabulae geographicae*, Duisburg, 1585.

The last map, 'Alpinae seu foederatae Rhaetiae', by the historian and statesman Fortunat Sprecher von Berneck (1585-1647) and Philippus Cluverius, was first issued by Willem Blaeu in 1618 and included in the *Atlantis Appendix*, 1630.[40]

VOLUME IX
Italy

This volume is composed entirely of maps of Italy to which country Joan Blaeu had also devoted the third volume of his *Theatrum* in 1640. There are only minor differences between the Italian volumes of 1640 and 1662. For the *Grand Atlas* and also for the Latin and Dutch editions the following new maps were made: (9) 'Corsica'; (42) 'Ducatus Braccianus'; (52) 'Insulae Tremitanae'. Map (9) superseded the old small-scale map of Corsica. Map (59) 'Sardinia' had already been added to the *Theatrum* in 1650. The third *Theatrum* volume comprised 58 maps of Italy and 4 maps of Greece, so that the *Grand Atlas* only included two more maps of Italy than the *Theatrum* did in 1640. The text likewise remained substantially unaltered. Blaeu had derived his maps and text in 1640 from the famous work of the Italian astronomer and geographer Giovanni Magini (1555-1617) whose *Italia* was posthumously printed at Bologna.[41] It was published in 1620 under the title, *Italia di Gio. Ant. Magini, data in luce da Fabio suo figliulo ... Bononiae, impensis ipsius auctoris 1620*, with text and 61 maps. Here again we find that practically no up-to-date maps were introduced into what was virtually an altas of forty-three years standing.

VOLUME X
Spain and Africa

In the part devoted to Spain, which included Portugal at the time the *Grand Atlas* was being published, we find 13 maps which had appeared in the *Theatrum* of 1640. We can analyse these maps as follows:

(1) Regnorum Hispaniae nova descriptio. Included in 1630 in Willem Jansz Blaeu's *Atlantes Appendix*.

(2), (10)-(13), (15), (23), (24), (25), (27) were issued in the first edition of the Theatrum in 1635.

(16) and (26) were included in *L'Appendice* of (1638).

The atlas was expanded in 1662 by the addition of 7 architectural drawings of the Escorial, sheets (3)-(9), and of maps (14), (17)-(22), and (28).

Joan Blaeu included all the maps of his earlier atlas in the *Atlas Maior*. Among them were items based on quite early originals such as map (10) 'Gallaecia Regnum' by Hermando Ojea (†1615) and map (21) 'Portugallia et Algarbia' by Fernando Alvaro Seco (1560-1600) dating from 1561.[42] The authors of the remaining early maps are not mentioned and their origin cannot now be traced. Most of the 9 maps added in 1662 are by the Portuguese cartographer Joao Baptista Lavanha (= L.B. Labanna). These are maps (18)-(22) dating from about 1615.[43]

The last map (28) was copied from a map engraved by the famous Portuguese cartographer Luis Teixeira, which Abraham Ortelius had already included in his *Theatrum* in 1584.[44]

Africa

In an analysis of the regional maps of Africa other criteria apply than in that of the European maps. There were no African cartographers and the representation by European cartographers was generally based on speculation. Except for its coastline, Africa was *terra incognita* in the 17th century, notwithstanding the depiction of rivers, places, and mountains in the interior on 16th- and 17th-century maps. The representations of Africa which appeared in the maps of Ptolemy (Claudius Ptolemeus, c. 87-150 A.D.) have been the subject of extensive study.[45] Their influence on 16th- and 17th-century cartographers was unmistakable.

In the 16th century separate maps of the African continent were issued by various authors[46]: Seb. Münster, 1540; G. B. Ramusio, 1550; G. Gastaldi, 1560; P. Forlani, 1562; A. Ortelius, 1570, and others. And in 1588 an atlas of twelve maps entirely devoted to Africa was published in Venice, the *Geografia di Livio Sanuto*, which was mainly based, however, on Ptolemy. The 16th-century regional maps of Africa showed Barbary, West Africa (the Kingdom of Congo), the land of Prester John, and South Africa.

This constellation underwent little change in the 17th century. It was not till late in the 17th century that the penetration of Africa by explorers resulted in more exact and more detailed information about the interior.[47] The atlases of the Blaeus only contained five maps of Africa until seven more were added to the *Atlas Maior* in 1662. One of the five early maps, the general map 'Africa nova descriptio . . .' dating from about 1620, was still being printed from the old plate in 1662. Maps (31) 'Ferrae et Matocchi' and (33) 'Aetopia Inferior' were engraved in 1635 after maps in the atlas of Hondius. The seven maps added by Blaeu in 1662 were entirely new. Maps (34) 'Nigritarum Regio' and (37) 'Regna Congo et Angola' in particular would have attracted attention at the time, since they gave more information than had been customary for these areas. The source of these maps is unknown, and this is also the case with the remaining five maps, none of which is signed.

VOLUME XI
Asia

In Asia lay the economic empire of the powerful Dutch East India Company of which Joan Blaeu was the cartographer. His inside information on the detailed maps in the files of the Company is not reflected, however, in the Asian volume of the *Grand Atlas*. Without the Atlas of China, which is virtually a separate entity, the maps of Asia would not have filled an entire volume of the *Grand Atlas*. After 1635 the Asian section of Blaeu's *Theatrum* comprised ten maps. In 1662 only one new map, (6) 'Arabia', was added.

Volume XI opens with the general map 'Asia noviter delineata' which had been issued by Willem Blaeu in or about 1620. Two maps, (5) 'Terra Sancta' and (10) 'Moluccae insulae', were printed from plates which Willem Blaeu had procured from Jodocus Hondius II in 1629. Map (9) 'Magni Mogolis Imperium' had been added to the *Theatrum* in 1638. The remaining maps had all been included in the first edition of the *Theatrum* in 1653.

It must be admitted that Joan Blaeu's original contribution to the cartography of Asia was extremely slight. On the other hand, he deserves credit for publishing the first European atlas of China.

The history of Chinese cartography is considerably older than the European. Apart from still earlier maps, the 'Mongol Atlas' deserves mention as the most significant monument of Chinese cartography. This atlas was compiled about 1311-1312 by Chu Ssu-pên. It contained maps of the provinces of the Chinese empire. It was this atlas (revised by Lo Hung-hsien) that was translated into Latin by the Jesuit Father Martin Martini (1614-1661).[48] And it was from Martini's atlas that Joan Blaeu derived his information for the *Atlas Sinensis*.

This atlas of Chu Ssu-pên (in the revision by Lo Hung-hsien) was later amended by other Chinese authors. A printed issue of 1615 is in the possession of the Royal Asiatic Society, London[49] and a practically identical copy is in the Museum Meermanno-Westreenianum at The Hague (see below).

In the reign of the emperor Kang-hsi new surveys of the Chinese empire were made by the Jesuit fathers. These surveys, which were much better than the former, provided the base for d'Anville's *Atlas de la Chine* of about 1730.

Though Joan Blaeu had issued the first European transcription of an atlas of China, the sources on which his work was based were outdated by the time of publication (1655). A revised edition was already in circulation by this time as we have pointed out above. Father Martin Martini was not the only one to transcribe Chinese maps in a European language. Cartographic work is known to us by the Polish sinologist Michael Boym (1612–1659). A manuscript atlas by him is preserved in the Vatican Library.[50] This atlas contains 18 maps (Blaeu's atlas has 17 maps, viz. 16 of China and one of Japan) which, like Father Martini's *Atlas Sinensis*, are founded on a printed version of the revised 'Mongol Atlas'. The Chinese atlas copied by the Jesuits in the 17th century was accompanied by a detailed text, a geographical description of China, *Ti t'u tsung yao*, from which the fathers borrowed extensively. A copy of this 'Chinese Geography', printed in 1643, is in the Vatican Library.[51] Szczesniak mentions that this text and the atlas were both presented to the Vatican Library by Philip Couplet on his visit to Rome in 1680. This information ties in well with contemporaneous information concerning the provenance of the Chinese atlas in the Museum Meermanno-Westreenianum at The Hague (115 B1), for the Jesuit father Philip Couplet had also presented Nicolaes Witsen with a copy of a Chinese atlas printed in the 17th century when he visited Amsterdam. Philip Couplet, a native of Mechlin, worked in China from 1656 to 1680. He was in Europe from 1683 to 1692 and he is known to have visited Amsterdam more than once in this period.[52]

The Chinese atlas in question bears the following annotation, dated 1684, in Witsen's handwriting:

'Father Philip Couplet gave me this Chinese atlas when he returned from China, where he had spent twenty-four years, to report in Rome on the situation of the Christian faith in that country. He also showed me another small Chinese atlas half the size of this, from which Martinus Martini had derived his atlas, as was evident from the annotations in Martini's own hand on the maps. He further said that the atlas from which Martini copied his maps had been compiled three hundred years earlier and that all the descriptions one reads in the Atlas of China can be easily traced word for word in the Chinese; these maps, however, His Reverence said, were quite new and much better.   N. Witsen, 1684.'

Witsen was referring, of course, to Blaeu's *Atlas Sinensis*. We can therefore establish that the source of Blaeu's atlas, viz.

Martini's work, was of an earlier date than the Chinese atlas in the museum at The Hague. Martin Martini was born at Trent and from 1637 onwards he worked as a Jesuit missionary in China. In 1651 he was at Rome. He then departed again for China where he died in 1661.[53] On 1 March 1654, Johan Bapt. Engelgrave authorized the printing of Martini's atlas.

Martin Martini's original atlas (presumably in manuscript with a Latin transcription of the Chinese topographical names) has not survived. The Latin translation was published separately (without maps) by Joan Blaeu. *Mart. Martinius, Sinicae historiae decas prima ... Amstelaedami, apud Joannem Blaeu*, in 1659 in small octavo.

Joan Blaeu had the seventeen maps in his atlas of China engraved after Martini's manuscript maps. If we compare Blaeu's maps with the atlas in the Museum Meermanno-Westreenianum (Couplet/Witsen) we notice the following points:

a) In both atlases the maps of the provinces fill a whole sheet. The maps in Blaeu's atlas are on a scale of 1 : 1,5 mill., about twenty per cent larger than those in the Chinese atlas.

b) In both atlases we find exactly the same areas represented on a sheet.

c) Blaeu's maps are richer in detail than the maps in the Chinese atlas. This implies that he must have worked after another model. We can therefore conclude that the Martini atlas on which Blaeu based his work differed in character from the Chinese atlas which Couplet had given Witsen, but that the arrangement in both Chinese atlases was similar and that the maps must also have been very similar.

A map of the province of Chekiang, measuring 32 × 33 cm, is reproduced here in illustration.

Father Martini's text is not, as Blaeu pointed out in his Preface to the Reader, an imitation of the geographical description mentioned above. It is an account, written in the first person, of the geography and history, the manners and customs of the Chinese empire and its peoples.

In his lengthy introduction Father Martini relates more than once how he compiled his maps from those of the Chinese. The profusion of data forced him to apply a stringent selection. Father Martini makes a distinction between Chinese and Tartar maps with reference to his sources. On p. 23 of the Dutch edition, for instance, we read:

Though I gladly and candidly admit that I have never seen these lands (i.e. Eastern Tartary) with my own eyes, I will nevertheless add to this account some information from the Chinese maps, and indeed even from those of the Tartars . . .

In his dedication to the Syndics of the Dutch East India Company in the Dutch edition of the *Atlas Sinensis* Blaeu mentions that Father Martini had written the Latin translation on the long voyage to Holland. He writes:

'Several reasons have compelled me, as it were, to dedicate this Chinese atlas (which I have translated into Dutch from the Latin text of the Rev. Martinus Martinius) to your honours . . .

. . . There is one reason, however, about which I cannot be silent, which is that this book of the Rev. Martinius was translated on board your ships, and so under your protection, from the Chinese language (which he has frequently read to us like his mother tongue) into Latin, and thus made available for the common good and for those who love learning and fine art.'

Blaeu was also convinced that the *Atlas Sinensis* would be advantageous to the Dutch East India Company. He probably had the trade relations in mind, as the atlas was not suitable for navigational purposes. The *Atlas Sinensis* was one of the remarkable cartographic achievements of the 17th century. With its maps of the Chinese provinces, it provided considerably more geographical information about China than was made available in the 18th and the 19th centuries. And even today we would find no European atlas providing sixteen maps of China to a scale of 1 : 1,5 mill.

Fourteen years after the publication of the *Atlas Sinensis* Joan Blaeu was approached by Philip Couplet with a proposal to print a historical description of China. There is evidence of this in a letter by Blaeu about which no further information is forthcoming:[54]

'Extract from a certain missive by Father Philippus Couplet, written from Canton on 24 January 1669 to Mr. Joan Blaeu resident in Amsterdam.

. . . This is to inform your honour that oneof our companions, by the name of Prosper Intercetta, is undertaking the voyage to Europe this year in order to have a very remarkable book, translated from Chinese into Latin, printed there. He has also taken with him a Chinese printer who is extremely skilled in writing Chinese lettering, in cutting or carving out in wooden blocks and finally in printing the Chinese characters; having been asked several times by whom this aforementioned book could be printed, we have unanimously recommended your honour's printing house, and the Atlas Sinicus of Master Martini of blessed memory provided a more than convincing confirmation of our good opinion . . .'

Joan Blaeu did not fall in with the proposal for the obvious reasons that the cutting of Chinese characters would involve all sorts of complications and that a historical treatise on the Chinese empire was already incorporated in his *Atlas Sinensis*.

As in the case of the Asian volume, Joan Blaeu had the opportunity to include in the American volume anything from ten to twenty maps that would have excited the interest of his contemporaries. Blaeu was the custodian of the detailed charts of the American coasts made by Joh. Vingboons for the Dutch East India Company. It was strictly forbidden, however, to publish this information. But even without utilizing this confidential material, Blaeu could have produced more maps of America. He omitted material that was available and satisfied himself with the heterogeneous assortment of twenty-three maps all told which make up volume XII.

In 1597 Cornelis Wytfliet had compiled an atlas of America with 19 maps, the *Descriptionis Ptolemaicae Augmentum*, in Louvain. In the years around 1660, when the Dutch colony of New Netherlands was flourishing, there was every reason to supply a more advanced cartographic presentation than the *Grand Atlas* actually did.

Shortly after the publication of the *Grand Atlas*, the first marine atlas, or rather pilot book, of the West Indies and North America appeared in print in Amsterdam. This was Arent Roggeveen's *Brandend Veen*, issued by Pieter Goos in 1675, which included 30 charts of the American coastline. Joan Blaeu, on the contrary, was content to reprint several old plates from his father's day, supplemented by four hitherto unpublished maps and a reprint of five plates of maps of Brazil that thad been engraved for Barlaeus's *Rerum per octeium in Brasilia gestarum historia*, Amsterdam, 1647.

We can analyse the maps in volume XII as follows:

(1) America nova tabula. Reprint of a plate used about 1620 by Willem Blaeu.

(4), (10)-(13), (22) and (23). These were the seven maps printed from the copper-plates procured by Willem Blaeu in 1629 from Jodocus Hondius II. In addition to these seven maps, Jodocus Hondius had sold four other plates of regional maps oj America to Willem Blaeu. These maps were included in early editions of Blaeu's atlas but not in the *Atlas Maior*. Jodocus Hondius had based his maps on those in Johannes de Laet's *Beschrijvinghe van West-Indien*, Amsterdam, 1625, which included the following maps:

1. Americae sive Indiae Occidentalis Tabula Generalis.
2. Maiores Minoresque Insulae. Hispaniola. Cuba Lucaiae et Caribes.
3. Nova Francia et Regiones Adiacentes.
4. Nova Anglia, Novum Belgium Et Virginia.
5. Florida, et Regiones Vicinae.
6. Nova Hispania, Nova Gallicia, Guatimala.
7. Terra Firma item Nuevo Reyno De Granada atque Popayan.
8. Peru.
9. Chili.
10. Provinciae Sitae Ad Fretum Magallanis itemque Fretum Le Maire.
11. Paraguay, O Prov. De Rio De La Plata: cum adiacentibus Provinciis. quas vocant Tucuman, Et S^{TA}. Cruz De La Sierra.
12. Provincia de Brasil cum Adiacentibus Provinciis.
13. Guaiana sive Provinciae intra Rio De Las Amazonas atque Rio De Yviapari sive Orinoque.
14. Venezuela, atque Occidentalis Pars Novae Andalusiae.

The relation between the maps in the *Grand Atlas* and those of De Laet and Hondius respectively can be traced as follows:
(3) Nova Belgica et Anglia Nova. Copied from De Laet and issued in 1635 by Willem Blaeu. This map later served as prototype of the famous maps 'New Netherlands' and 'New Eng-

land' by C. J. Visscher and Joh. Janssonius respectively. They introduced new features to the map, adding, for instance, the lovely view of 'Nieuw Amsterdam op 't Eylant Manhattans'.[55]

(4) Nova Virginia Tabula. Copper-plate by Jodocus Hondius II, engraved after the map of John Smith, 1606.

(10) Mappa Aestiuarum Insularum, alias Bermudas dictarum. Copper-plate by Jodocus Hondius II, after De Laet.

(11) Terra Firma et Novum Regnum Gravatense et Popayan. Idem.

(12) Peru. Idem.

(13) Chile. Idem.

(22) Guiana sive Amazonum Regio. Idem.

(23) Venezuela cum parte Australi Nova Andalusiae. Idem.

The sources of the remaining maps are as follows:[56]

(5) 'Virginia partis australis' and (16) 'Brasilia' were first issued in 1638 (?) in the *Appendice*. The map 'Virginis partis australis' is based on an early map by Jodocus Hondius 'Virginiae Item et Floridae Americae', dating from 1606 (for a detailed description of Blaeu's additions cf. Cumming, p. 138). The map 'Brasilia' superseded the early Hondius map 'Novus Brasiliae typus'.

(6) 'Nova Hispania et Nova Galicia', (8) 'Insulae Americanae in Oceano Septentrionali', (14) 'Tabula Magellanica . . .' had been included in Willem Blaeu's *Theatrum* in 1635. With the exception of (8), these plates were engraved after the maps of De Laet.

(17)-(21) were the maps which derived, as we have mentioned above, from Barlaeus's *Brasilia*. This leaves maps (2), (7), (9), and (15) which were specially engraved for the *Atlas Maior*.

23. 'Dominico Fiorentino'. From G. A. Magini's *Italia*, 1620. Copied by Willem Jansz. Blaeu in the third

6. The fire

Under the prevailing climatic conditions, February is the coldest month of the year in Holland. The low temperatures recorded in this month are due to cold air currents from the East, frequently accompanied by continuous easterly gales. As Dutch houses are not adapted to excessive cold, indoor temperature is liable to drop pretty close to outdoor level unless equally excessive heating is available. In direct relation with these circumstances is the high February frequency of fires which are extremely difficult to control and localize owing to the strong easterly wind. Several catastrophic fires are recorded in Dutch history in which large and prominent buildings have gone up in flames in the month of February.

The fire of 22/23 February 1672 at the Gravenstraat press of the Blaeus occurred in circumstances similar to those which prevail even at the present time. We will confine ourselves to reproducing a few contemporary accounts recording the cause, magnitude, and damage of the disaster.

Our first item is a report of the fire in the well-known annual chronicle *Hollandse Mercurius*:[57]

'A chill easterly wind had been blowing incessantly, causing severe cold and dryness. The Alderman Johan Blaeuw is reported to have owned one of the finest printing houes in Amsterdam at this time; to which I add that this is beyond dispute. Heaven ordained the disaster that on the 23 of this month at half-past three in the night, due to the drying of firewood, or indeed negligence

93

24. Contemporary carved wooden cabinet, specially designed for Blaeu's
Atlas Maior, now in the Amsterdam University Library.

of the apprentices, this magnificent printing house caught fire and that with it type, presses, plates and paper (flakes of which went flying as far as the Amsterdam Toll-gate) were burnt, scorched, destroyed and so damaged that one . . . regrets the plates of the Atlas, the towns of these countries, the mechanical and other technical plates, documents, etc. which were partly ruined and spoiled by the fire.'

A more or less official report on the fire by the fire-brigade officer Jan van der Heiden is to be found in his book on the new fire-extinguisher:[58]

'Though this damage was considerable, that caused by the next fire, the first in the year 1672, was even much greater. It occurred in the frosty night of 22 February in the letterpress and copper-plate printing house of Mr. Joan Blauw near the Nieuwe Kerk; being right in the centre of town, a large number of the old fire-extinguishers were soon at hand and put to work, but just as soon were frozen and useless . . . the fire penetrated wherever no open spaces or double walls existed. Several outbuildings at the rear burnt down besides the entire premises and stock of the shop. In addition, the large printing works with everything in it was damaged to such an extent that even the copper-plates stacked in the far corners melted like lead in the flames and others were completely scorched. A large number of very important plates were lost there . . . The considerable damage caused hereby is conservatively estimated by the owners:

to buildings at	27,000 guilders
to plates, equipment and other goods in printing works and shop premises	355,000 guilders
sum total	382,000 guilders'

The third report is from the well-known publisher Daniel Elsevier to his Antwerp colleague Moretus in a letter written on 4 March:

'Mr. Blau's loss is great. All the plates were in the fire and are considerably damaged. Many, however, are being restored and there is hope that more than two-thirds or three-quarters of the total will be restored . . .What he has lost is the building, all the presses with their appurtenances, 4 to 5000 reams of blank paper for printing, about 5000 printed sheets of Grotius and N. Test., 5 to 6000 practically fully printed, and certainly 40000 pounds of type, of which 16000 pounds of metal have been recovered; and if there had been no water, all his books would also have been burnt and the consequent loss in my opinion twice as heavy. I believe that the good gentleman has lost about 60 to 70 thousand guilders . . .'

The reports do not quite agree. In the first place, there is the question of the extent of the damage. Jan van der Heiden mentions a sum of 382,000 guilders, Daniel Elsevier a 'mere' 60 or 70 thousand guilders. Secondly, it is evident from Van der Heiden's report that the copper-plates were totally lost. According to Elsevier, however, three-quarters of them could still be used despite the damage. Be that as it may, the fire precipitated the end of the publishing house of the Blaeus, the more so since Joan Blaeu died the next year. The activities of the Blaeus after 1672 are discussed in the final chapter of this introduction.

7. Further history of the Atlas Maior

The fire at the Gravenstraat premises on 22/23 February 1672 had destroyed large stocks of printed books and atlases. The press on Bloemgracht, however, remained in operation, and business was conducted as usual at the shop 'op 't Water'. When Dr. Joan Blaeu died the next year, the firm lost its leader, which was one of the main factors contributing to the gradual liquidation of the house of Blaeu.

The stock of books and copper-plates was disposed of in a series of sales. First sale, 23 April 1674: books only. Second sale, 14 May 1674: all the books, the Atlas and town atlases excepted. Third sale, 28 August 1674: Atlases, town atlases of the Netherlands and Italy with the plates. Fourth sale, 20 April 1677: books, maps, copper-plates, etc. Fith sale, 26 April 1677: books only.

The greater part of the stock must have been acquired by the bookseller Abraham Wolfgang who acted in partenership with the booksellers Boom, Van Waesbergen, and Van Someren. Abraham Wolfgang had also procured stock and copper-plates of Janssonius's atlases in 1675.[59]

On 28 March 1674 six leading Amsterdam booksellers entered into an agreement, one of the reasons for their association being to prevent, in the event of the decease on one of them, the books in the estate from being sold for a mere song.[60] The six parties to the agreement were Joh. Janssonius Van Waesbergen, Daniel Elsevier, Johannes van Someren, Abraham Wolfgang, Hendrick and Dirck Boom. Van Eeghen rightly concludes that the association had been inspired by the circumstances attending the sales of Joan Blaeu who had died recently. The said associates agreed that each of the surviving parties would buy at least 1/32 of the assessed value of the estate if one of their number died.

Notwithstanding the above-mentioned sales, new editions of the town atlases of Piedmont and Savoy were issued by the Blaeu heirs in 1682 and 1693, and a volume of the *Atlas Maior* by John Blaeu the younger in 1680, the latter being presumably compiled from existing stock (cf. *Atlantes Neerlandici*, p. 56 A).

Albert Magnus (1642-1689), the famous bookbinder, likewise procured a number of the maps, atlases, and globes. Various advertisements in newspapers lead us to assume that, next to Abraham Wolfgang, Magnus, and after 1689 his widow, was the most important dealer in Blaeu atlases.

Advertisements (K. & S. pp. 400-401):

1678. Opr. Haarlemmer Courant no. 19: announcement of the globes, etc. of the later Joan Blaeu offered for sale.

1685. Opr. Haarlemmer Courant no. 13: Atlases in Latin, French, German, and Dutch from the stock of the late Mr. Joan Blaeu are obtainable at Albert Magnus's.

1691. Opr. Haarlemmer Courant no. 16: On 25 April the widow of Albert Magnus will sell the stock of the bookshop as well as the atlases and town atlases of the late Mr. Joan Blaeu.

1693. Amsterd. Courant, 5 February: The heirs of Albert Magnus are selling, at a modest price, the original and complete atlases by Mr. Joan Blaeu . . .as well as the town atlases of the Netherlands, Italy, Savoy, Piedmont, etc.

1707. Amsterdam. Courant, 12 March: The heirs of the late widow of Albert Magnus will sell all the books left, bound and unbound, among which are many atlases by Blaeu and Janssonius in various languages. In particular, an atlas in Latin by Blaeu in 19 volumes, delightfully illuminated by Dirk Jansz van Santen.

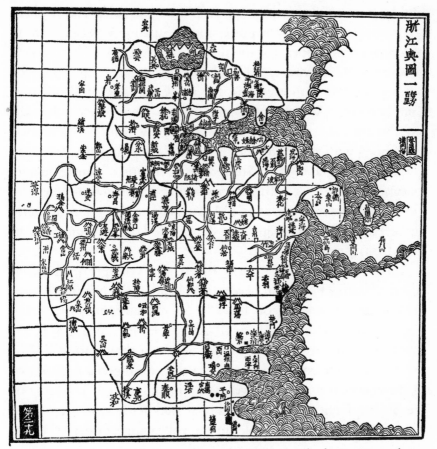

25. The province of Chekiang from the Chinese Atlas by Lo Hung-hsien, presented to Nic. Witsen by L. Couplet. (See p. 85)

Others, including private persons, purchased several copies of the *Atlas Maior* at various sales. One of these was Paulus van Uchelen, whose collection comprised fifteen copies as witnessed by the sales catalogue of 1703.[61] In 1672 another Amsterdam bibliophile, Goswinus Uilenbroek, procured eight copies of the Spanish *Atlas Maior* damaged by water and fire, from which he was able to compile one sound complete copy.[62]

On 25 June 1678 the shop 'op 't Water' was sold (Van Eeghen, III, p. 23), passing into the possession of Susanna Veselaer, widow of Jan Jacob Schepper, for the sum of Fl. 13,500.—. The press on Bloemgracht, however, was still in full operation, printing for other publishers, among them for the Company of Wolfgang, Van Someren, Waesbergen, and Boom. Joan Blaeu II himself later became an associate of the Company. We find books printed at his press with the following imprints: 'Amstelodanie, Ex typographia Blaviana 1682 ...Sumptibus societatis'; 'Amstelodanie, ex typographia P. et J. Blaeu, prostant apud Janssonio-Waesbergios, Boom et Goethals, 1701'; 'A Amsterdam, Dans l'imprimerie de G. P. et J. Blaeu, 1686, Aux dépens de la Compagnie', (Van Eeghen, III, p. 24).

After the death of Dr. Joan Blaeu, the younger Joan Blaeu (then 22 years of age) had become the head of the printing house, but the chief printer Jacob Lescaille (cf. Van Eeghen, III, p. 24) acted as works manager. Joan Blaeu II, who is recorded as being an advocate by profession, was not active in the printing side of the business. He confined himself to the commercial interests of the firm until it was finally wound up in 1694-1696. The fame of the Bloemgracht press continued unabated in the years after 1672. This is reflected, for example, in the following verses:[63]

Op 't zien van de Drukkerij van de Heeren Blau:

Hier ben ik in den BLAUWEN hemel,
Daar 't drie-tal Broed'ren, Goden zijn,
Bewegers van dit groot gewemel;
Hier perst me uit lett'ren starreschijn,
't Geen 't menschdom meedeeld, ligt en luister
Gelijk de Zon aan Maan en Starr';
Hier zie ik voor 't onwetend duister,

Drie Starre in 't hemels BLAU, van varr':
Staâ vast! ik dwaal, het zijn drie Zonnen,
Drie Zoonen, van den grooten BLAU,
Die zulke Starren scheppen konnen,
Welk straalen tot in 't kabel grauw,
Van al des weerelds drifte kielen,
Daar al wie Zee bond, streek naar zet,
En steets ontel'bre duizend zielen,
Van klip, van zand, en stranden red;
Hier schept men 't ligt, voor de onderzoeker,
O weerelds wond're Drukkerij!

In 1694 there was a large sale, at Wolfgang's, of atlases and copper-plates from the stock of the Blaeus (K. & S. 1019) and on 7 April 1695 the printing equipment which still comprised nine presses was sold (K. & S. 52, 53). Curiously enough, books with the imprint of P. and J. Blaeu were being printed after the sale, such as, in 1699, volumes I and II of *M. Tillii Ciceronis Orationes . . .*' Amstelodami, Ex typographia P. & I. Blaeu, Prostant apud Janssonio-Waesbergios, Boom, à Someren, & Goethals' (Van Eeghen III, p. 25).

But after the sale of the printing office in 1695, the Company had to have their printing done elsewhere. They presumably divided their work between various Amsterdam printers. Van Eeghen (III, p. 26) mentions Johannes Steenbergen in this context. The Blaeu brothers, Pieter and Joan II, continued to have a hand in publishing various books after 1695 as partners in the Company. Though the printing house of Blaeu had ceased to exist, the Company retained the printer's mark of the Blaeus in several books as late as 1703 (Van Eeghen, III, p. 26). The Company was dissolved on 3 July 1706. But in 1713 a reprint of an *Histoire du Concile de Trente* was issued with the imprint 'A

Amsterdam Dans l'imprimerie de G. P. et J. Blaeu, 1713. Aux dépens de la Compagnie' (Van Eeghen, id.). In 1708 Joan Blaeu II retired from the book trade. He resigned from the guild and disposed of his share of the book stock (K. & S. p. 924).

The maps outlasted the firm, because the copper-plates, insofar as they had not been damaged by the fire in 1672, had been sold to various printers. Pieter Mortier acquired the plates of the town atlases of Italy, Frederik de Wit those of the Netherlands. But it is not so easy to find out to whom the atlas maps went. It is very likely that Pieter Mortier also acquired a number of the atlas plates which later passed to Covens & Mortier. In the map catalogue of Covens & Mortier we can trace 65 Blaeu maps and the maps from the atlas of China. From the contents of the Ottens atlases it can be deduced that this firm had likewise acquired a number of Blaeu plates. The worn plates still show Blaeu's imprint and not that of Ottens. Blaeu maps are also found in atlases published by Carel Allard but these may be from old stock. It is very probable that Frederick de Wit likewise printed atlas maps from plates deriving from Blaeu via Wolfgang. The assertion, however, that Schenk & Valck re-issued the Blaeu maps (Bagrow) should be refuted. Schenk & Valck procured the plates of the *Novus Atlas* of Janssonius.

In 1708 we find an Amsterdam publisher Christiaan Vermeij requesting from the City Council a license to issue octavo reprints of the text of the Dutch, French, and Latin editions of the *Atlas Maior*. The officers of the Booksellers' Guild advised the Council not to grant the request, since 'the same officers could not understand how the suppliant could have made such a request, as it is quite well known to him that the plates and books and the right to print the same had been sold by the heirs of the late Mr. Blaeuw to several booksellers in the country . . .'[64]

Material circumstances as much as intellectual qualities determined a person's eligibility for the magistracy of the powerful city of Amsterdam. By virtue of their wealth, Dr. Joan Blaeu and his children belonged to the circle of patricians whose luxurious way of life stamped the era in which they lived as the Golden Age. Despite the disastrous fire, Dr. Joan Blaeu left his heirs a substantial fortune which was further increased by the capital of their equally wealthy spouses. Both his sons and daughters had married well. The collateral inheritance at the decease of the first wife of Joan Blaeu II in 1704 exceeded Fl. 96,000.[65] The second husband of his daughter Louise was a well-to-do merchant whose taxable capital in 1674 was Fl. 140,000.[66]

Like their father, Dr. Blaeu's sons filled various public offices. Joan Blaeu II was a member of the Council from 1695 until his death in 1712. In 1690 he had been elected alderman. He became a Captain of the Civic Guard in 1693 and a Syndic of the Dutch East India Company in 1705.[67] Willem Blaeu was an advocate and owner of the manor 'Het Hof' at Hillegom. According to Elias[68], he had also followed in his father's footsteps as member of the Council and had likewise been relieved of his post by Prince William III. He is recorded as Captain of the Civic Guard in 1663.

When his father died, Joan Blaeu II played a leading role in the publishing firm, evincing a special interest in cartography. In his correspondence with the Swedish scholar J. G. Sparvenfelt, 1688-1695[69], map publishing is repeatedly mentioned. We also find a reference in these letters to Joan's residence 'à la campagne'. In 1695 he acquired a house on Herengracht which was sold after his death to Jan Jacob de Famars for the sum of Fl. 37,240.[70]

Pieter Blaeu was entrusted with the management of the bookshop 'op 't Water'. He was a Lieutenant of the Civic Guard in

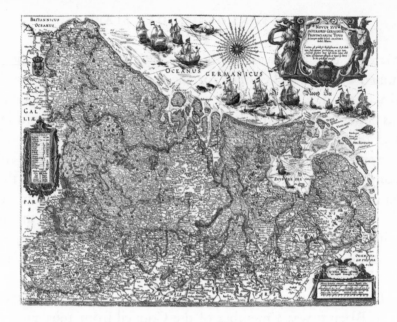

26. Map of The Netherlands, from Joan Blaeu's *Toonneel des Aerdrycx*, 1642.

Dr. Joan Blaeu, 1598-1673 + Geertruid Vermeulen

Mr. Joan Blaeu, 1650-1712
1. + 6-7-1679, Eva van Neck (1656-1704)
2. + 1-9-1705, Elisabeth van Thije (1672-1706)
3. + 2-12-1707, Maria Sautijn (1671-1748)

Mr. Willem Blaeu, 1635-1685
+ 1659, Anna van Loon

26a. Genealogy of the Blaeu family.

28. Scheme of the publication of land atlases by the Blaeus.

1630	1631	
Atlantis appendix sive pars altera . . .	*Appendix Theatri A. Ortelii et Atlantis G. Mercatoris . . .*	*Novu Theat Terra volum ed. in Frenc Latin*

27. Map of the province of (North- and South-) Holland, from Willem Jansz. Blaeu's *Novus Atlas*, 1635.

1640	1645	1654	1655	1662
The Theatrum in 3 vol.: 1640 ed. in French and Latin, 1642 in Dutch and German. The added vol. contains Italy	*The Theatrum in 4 vol.: 1645 ed. in Latin, French and German, 1646 in Dutch. The added vol. contains England and Ireland*	*The Theatrum in 5 vol.: 1654 ed. in French, German, Dutch and Latin. The added vol. contains Scotland*	*The Theatrum in 6 vol.: 1655 ed. in French, German, Dutch and Latin. The added vol. contains China*	*Atlas Major with Latin text in 11 vol. (1662), French text in 12 vol. (1663), Dutch text in 9 vol. (1664) and Spanish text in 10 vol. (1672)*

1679, was appointed recorder of the Orphan Chamber in 1668 and dike-reeve of the Nieuwer Amstel polder in 1694. From 1693 onwards he occupied a house on Herengracht, spending the summers at his manor-house 'Sonnesteijn' on the Amstel. Pieter Blaeu was very active in the book trade in which he was already prominent in his father's time. The maintenance of relations with Italy appears to have mainly devolved on him. His letters to Italian authorities in the period 1660-1695 have been preserved, among them a fairly extensive correspondence with de Medici· As a printer of Roman Catholic church-books, Pieter Blaeu was well-known throughout Europe (see below) and in the years around 1690 the fame of the atlases and maps was still great enough to merit mention in Leti's *Teatro Belgico* (see Appendix). Joan II and Pieter Blaeu remained active in publishing till late in life (the association with Van Someren, Boom, etc. was dissolved after Pieter Blaeu's death in 1706) but with the death of Joan II in 1712 their name vanished definitively from the world of print. This had nothing to do with the fire of 1672, for the printing house had continued to flourish long after that event. The discontinuance of the firm should probably be attributed to a lack of interest in the younger generation and the absence of a successor to Joan Blaeu II.

The name Blaeu is frequently recorded in Amsterdam in the 18th century, particularly in the world of commerce, but other printers and publishers were responsible for maintaining the typographical tradition of Amsterdam in the 18th and the 19th century. To conclude with the words of Prof. H. de la Fontaine Verwey:[71] 'The name of Blaeu represents a great episode in the history of our city and our country. This name is associated with every aspect of the political, economic, scholarly, and literary scene at the time in which the United Republic and Amsterdam achieved greatness.'

Appendix

From: G. Leti, *Teatro Belgico*. Amsterdam, 1690 (II, pp. 414-416)

Ogni qualunque arte, o mestiere ancora in questa Città ha una specie di Compagnia, con i suoi Giurati, per regolar gli interessi che occorrono nella propria arte, e quando uno di tal societá muore tutti gli altri son tenuti a portarsi per accompagnare il Cadavero alla sepoltura, altramente son tenuti ad un' emenda. Ma come non vi é mestiere che sia più numeroso, di quello della Libraria, e che ha più bisogno d'un buon regolamento, per questo vi si sono portati i rimedi nicessarii. Certo é che non vi é Città nel Mondo dove meglio fiorisce questa nobil' Arte, come in Amsterdamo. Si sa che il defunto Signor *Pietro Bleau*, Padre de' fratelli viventi intraprese opere che fecero maravigliare l'Universo, e ne son Testimonio i suoi Atlanti che servirono ad ogni modo per disgratia di questa Casa assai antica nell' ordine Patritio di cibo alle fiamme, sino alle Rame istesse, ancorche carissimi divennero poi quei pochi esemplarii che scapparono dall' incendio; non lascia peró il Signor Giovanni Bleau suo figliuolo, capacissimo delle più alte Magistrature, e di maggiori impieghi, e fratello del Signor Segretario di questo nome che veramente merita molto per essere esperto nelle Lingue, e nelle Lettere, e negli interessi generali, e particolarimente in quelli della Patria; non lascia per questo di conservare la piú fioritissima stamperia di tutto il Paese, con dieci Torchi, & un gran numero di scelti Operarii, e di dove escon le opere a lettere rosse che sono di maggiore stima tra Catolici.

Innumerabili sono ancora le Carte Geografiche che si stampano alla giornata in questa Città, e di tutto quello che riguarda alla sfera, alla marina, & alle cose terrestre, e maritime, e benche molti siano quei che fanno lavorare in ciò, e che vanno riunendo Atlanti in ogni perfettione, in ogni qualunque volume, e grandi, e piccioli, con tutto ciò é certissimo che tengono il maggior grido le Tavole, Carte Geografiche, & inumerabili figure, ch'escono dalle Stamperie del Signor *Nicolo Wischer* che in fatti, é la gentilezza istessa, e che con gran cortesia tratta con quei che hanno da far con esso lui; & ancora di quella del Signor *With*, di Religione Catolico, che fà pure gran negotio in materie di questa natura tanto di Carte che di figure curiose.

Ma per quello che spetta la libraria, dirò in generale, che il numero é quasi infinito de' Mercanti Librari, poiche per tutti gli angoli non si vede altro, ma fuori una dozena in circa al piú, del resto le facende son picciole. Molti sono ancora gli Stampatori, e per il governo di tutti insieme, per le cose che possono arriuare nelle materie di Libraria vi si stabiliscono de' Giurati innanzi a' quali si regolano tutti gli affari all' amichevole potendosi, altramente si recorre alla giustitia. La Carta é cara, e pure si stampa molto, e come il vivere è caro rispetto alle Taglie ben grandi, non possono che riuscir carissime l'impressioni, con tutto ció li libri sono a buonissimo Mercato, e ció nasce perche i librari, si contentano d'un certo guadagno mediocre, e quei che stampano hoggi lo vorebbono vender dimane per cosi dire, Altre volte le Stampe straniere erano rarissime, non facendosi altra professione che di stampar libri della lingua del Paese, o in Latino: ma da qualche tempo in quà non si vede uscir dalle Stampe che continue voragini di libri Francesi, e ben pochi in Italiano, anzi niuno se non fossero le mie opere. Sono infiniti ancora quei che lavorano in Rame, che però si veggono uscire alla luce in questa Città. molti libri, molto ben' arrichiti di figure, essendo molto portato a tal curiosità il genio Tedesco, & il Fiamengo. Non si trova quasi niuno Mercante libraro, che faccia professione di haver per suo uso Stamperia, come si vede in altri Regni, costumandosi di laíciar tale impiego. a' proprii Mercanti Stampatori.

Fanno grau figura nella libraria in questa Città li Signori *Giovanni Bleau, Abramo Wolfgang, Giovanni, & Egidio Janssonio à Waesberge, Henrico Boom, e la Signora Vedova di Theodoro suo fratello. Abrame a Someren, e Ramberto Goethals.* Questi Signori con grandissima spesa, hanno fatto stampare un numero infinito di buoni libri Latini, e per questo d'ordinario vien chiamata la Conpagnia della latinità. Li libri che si stampano si mettono tutti in un Magazeno, e ciascuno piglia quelli che ha bisogno per la sua Bottega alla giornata fattosi già il prezzo del Libro, enotato il tutto dal Direttore, nel sine dell'anno fattosi il conto, ciascuno paga puntualmente quello che ha preso, in danaro contante, che si mette in Cascia, e da questo danaro poi, si fanno le spese d'altre stampe. Sopra tutto fanno risplendere le stampe di Lettera rossa all' uso della Chiesa Romana, che per esser di ottima stampa se ne spacciano in tutte le parti del Mondo. Vi sono poi altre Compagnie di due, e di tre, che unite stampano pure ottimi Libri in ogni lingua, e si può dir che queste Compagnie nelle quali s'ammira ottima l'unione, sono di gran giovamento alla Città, poiche tanto in quello che fanno stampare in nome della Compagnia, come nel loro particolare, ciascuno da per se, é cosa certa che danno a vivere alla giornata nella sola Provincia d'Holanda a più di 800. perfone; siano fattori di Carta, Stampatori, Riligatori, Operari in Rame, Stampatori in Rame, Portatori, Collationatori, & altri in altre specie di Lavori; e benche sembra che in Amsterdamo il negotio della Libraria sia quafi il minimo, a causa che i Librari non vannomolto a far figura alla Borsa; con tutto ciò é certo che senza disprezzare gli altri, non vi é alcuna Arte, che dia a vivere alla giornata & a cosi gran numero di persone, come la Libraria, che quasi non puó credersi.

Notes

1. J. E. Elias, *De Vroedschap van Amsterdam*. 2 vol., Haarlem, 1903-1905, p. 472.

2. H. de la Fontaine Verwey, 'Het werk van de Blaeu's'. *Maandblad Amstelodamum*, 39 (1952), p. 102.

3. Rijksmuseum, Amsterdam.

4. Municipal Archives Amsterdam, Not. Arch. 2490, fol. 385; Nots. Jac. Hellerus.

5. M. M. Kleerkoper & W. P. van Stockum Jr., *De boekhandel te Amsterdam, vnl. in de 17e eeuw*. 's-Gravenhage, 1914-1916, p. 42.

6. Lloyd A. Brown, *The story of maps*. Boston, 1949, p. 172.

7. Municipal Archives Amsterdam, Not. Arch. 3014/197.

8. Kleerkoper & Van Stockum, p. 1162.

9. Municipal Archives Amsterdam, Not. Arch. 1959/20-20; Nots. David Doornick.

10. J. Keuning, 'Een reusachtige aardglobe van Joan Blaeu uit het midden der zeventiende eeuw'. *Tijdschrift Aardrijkskundig Genootschap*, LII (1935), pp. 525-538.

11. L. Bagrow, 'A Dutch Globe at Moscow, ca. 1650'. *Imago Mundi*, XIII (1956), p. 161.

12. L. Bagrow, 'The Gottorp Globe in Russia'. *Imago Mundi*, VI (1949), pp. 95-96.

13. National Library of Scotland, Edinburgh.

14. F. C. Wieder, *Monumenta Cartographica*. 1925-1933, pp. 84-85

15. National Library of Scotland, Edinburgh.

16. R. V. Tooley, *Maps and Map-makers*. London, 1952, p. 40.

17. R. A. Skelton, *County atlases of the British Isles*. Map Collectors' Series, no. 41, London, 1968, p. 113.

18. Facsimile reproduction by Theatrum Orbis Terrarum Ltd., Amsterdam, 1967.

19. From: C. Koeman, *Collections of maps and atlases in the Netherlands*. Leiden, 1961.

20. *Bibliotheca Uilenbroukiana sive catalogus Librorum* ... Amsterdam, 1729.

21. C. Koeman, 'Turkse transkripties van 17e-eeuwse Nederlandse atlassen'. *Bonacker Festschrift*, Bad Godesberg, 1968, pp. 71-76.

22. J. L. E. Dreyer, 'Tychonis Brahe Dani Opera'. *Havniae*, 1913-28, IX, p. 140.

23. H. Richter, 'W. J. Blaeu with Tycho Brahe on Hven and his map of the island'. *Imago Mundi* III (1939), pp. 53-60.

24. N. Friberg, 'A province map of Dalecarlia by Andreas Bureus (?)'. *Imago Mundi* XV (1960), pp. 73-83.

25. Friberg, op. cit. — S. Lönberg, *Sveriges Karta*. Uppsala, 1903. — J. Faggot, *Historien om Svenska Landmäteriet*. Stockholm, 1747.

26. C. Koeman, 'Some new contributions to the knowledge of Blaeu's atlases'. *Tijdschrift Aardrijkskundig Genootschap*, LXXVII (1960), pp. 278-286.

27. K. Buczek, *The History of Polish Cartography from the 15th to the 18th century*. Cracow and Warsaw, 1966.

28. W. Bonacker, *Kartenmacher aller Länder und Zeiten*. Stuttgart, 1966.

29. S. J. Fockema Andreae & B. van 't Hoff, *Geschiedenis der Kartografie van Nederland*. Den Haag, 1947.

30. Fockema Andreae & Van 't Hoff, op. cit., p. 39.

31. W. Bonacker, op. cit.

32. Fockema Andreae & Van 't Hoff, op. cit., p. 47.

33. R. A. Skelton, *County Atlases of the British Isles, 1579-1850*. Map Collectors' Series, No. 14, London, 1965.

34. Map Collectors' Series, No. 41, London, 1968, pp. 97-103. — D. G. Moir and R. A. Skelton, 'New Light on the first atlas of Scotland'. *Scottish Geographical Magazine*, vol. 84, no. 3 (Dec. 1968), pp. 149-159.

35. R. A. Skelton, *County Atlases ..., 1579-1850*. Map Collectors' Series, No. 14, London, 1965, p. 104.

36. C. Koeman, 'The Theatrum Universae Galliae, 1631'. *Imago Mundi*, XVII (1963), pp. 62-73.

37. F. de Dainville S. J., 'Le premier atlas de France.' *Actes du 85me Congrès National des Sociétés Savantes, section de géographie*. (Imprimerie Nationale), Paris, 1961 (extrait). See also de Dainville's *Introduction* to the facsimile edition of the *Théatre françois*. (Theatrum Orbis Terrarum Ltd.), Amsterdam, 1967.

38. F. de Dainville S. J., *L'évolution de l'Atlas de France sous Louis XIII. Théatre géographique du Royaume de France. Actes du 87me Congrès National des Sociétés Savantes, section de géographie*. (Imprimerie Nationale), Paris, 1963 (extrait).

39. F. de Dainville, op. cit., 1963.

40. W. Blumer, *Bibliographie der Gesamtkarten der Schweiz*. Bern, 1957, p. 163.

41. R. Almagià, *L'Italia di G. A. Magini e la cartografia dell'Italia nei secoli XVI e XVII*.

42. A. Cortesao, *Portugaliae Monumenta Cartographica*. Lisboa, 1960, vol. II, pp. 79-83.

43. A. Cortesao, op. cit., vol. IV, pp. 63-71.

44. A. Cortesao, op. cit., vol. III, p. 65.

45. Youssouf Kamal, *Monumenta Cartographica Africae et Aegypty*, 16 vols. with text. Ed. by Dr. F. C. Wieder. Cairo-Leiden, 1926-1951. See the complete contents of this work in *List of Atlases in the Library of Congress*, vol. 6, 1963, no. 19990.

46. F. A. Ogunsheye, 'Maps of Africa, 1500-1800, a bibliographic Survey'. *Nigerian Geographical Journal*, Ibadan, 7 (1964), p. 34-42.

47. R. V. Tooley, *Printed maps of the Continent of Africa*. Map Collectors' Series, Nos. 29 & 30, London, 1966.

48. Walter Fuchs, *The 'Mongol Atlas' of China by Chu Ssu-pên and the Kuang-yü-t'u* (i.e. the revision by Lo Hung-skien). With 48 facsimile maps dating from about 1555, pp. 32, pl. 48. Fu Jen University, Peiping, 1946. Monumenta Serica. Monograph 8.

49. W. Huttmann, 'On Chinese and European Maps of China'. *Journal of the R.G.S*, XIV (1844), pp. 117-127. Reprinted in *Acta Cartographica*, II, Amsterdam, 1968, pp. 235-244.

50. B. Szczesniak, 'The Mappa Imperii Sinarum of Michel Boym.' *Imago Mundi*, XIX (1965), pp. 113-115.

51. Szczesniak, op. cit.

52. A. de Backer, *Biblioth. des Ecrivains de la Compagnie de Jésus*, tome I.

53. A. de Backer, op. cit., tome II, p. 391.

54. A. van Lommel S. J. in *De Navorscher*, 1870, pp. 561-565.

55. I. N. Phelps Stokes, *The Iconography of Manhattan Island, 1498-1909.* 6 vols., New York, 1915-1928. (See list of maps and the reproductions in vol. II, 1916).

56. W. Cumming, *The Southeast in early maps.* Princetown, 1958.

57. *De Hollandse Mercurius, behelsende de aenmaerckelijckste Geschiedenissen voorgevallen over den gantschen Aerdtbodem, in den Jare 1672 tot 1673.* Haerlem, Pieter Casteleyn, 1673, p. 14.

58. Jan van der Heiden, *Beschrijving der nieuwelijks uitgevonden en geoctroyeerde slang-brand-spuiten en haare wijze van Brand-Blussen.* T' Amsterdam, By Jan Rieuwertsz . . ., 1690, p. 15.

59. M. M. Kleerkooper & W. P. Van Stockum Jr. *De Boekhandel te Amsterdam.* 's-Gravenhage, 1914-1916, p. 1018.

60. I. H. van Eeghen, *De Amsterdamse Boekhandel, 1680-1725.* Amsterdam, 1960-1966, IV, p. 158.

61. 'Catalogue of the fine collection of art and books of the late Mr. Paulus van Uchelen . . . with an appendix mainly of atlases and town atlases by the late Mr. Blaeu . . . which will be put up for sale on Monday the first of October 1703 and following days, at Amsterdam, at the residence of deceased . . . at Amsterdam by Hendrik Wetstein, where the catalogue is obtainable.'

62. This is mentioned in the Introduction of the Catalogue of the sale of the book collection of G. Uilenbroek: *Bibliotheca Uilenbroukiana sive catalogus Librorum* . . ., Amstelaedami, apud Westenios & Smith, 1729.

63. D. Schelte, *Rijm-werken.* Amsterdam, Hendrik Schelte, 1714, p. 989. Cf. Tiele en Dozy in: *Bijdragen Gesch. v. d. Boekh.*, V, 2, pp. 339, 352.

64. Requests 1629-1725, Booksellers Guild, Municipal Archives, Amsterdam. (Cf. also Kleerkooper & Van Stockum, op. cit., p. 53).

65. Van Eeghen, op. cit., III, p. 22.

66. J. E. Elias, *De Vroedschap van Amsterdam.* Haarlem, 1903-1905, p. 473.

67. Elias, op. cit.

68. Elias, op. cit.

69. Stiftsbibliotheek (Chapter Library), Linköpivy. Published in Kleer-kooper & Van Stockum, op. cit., pp. 46-56.

70. Van Eeghen, op. cit, III, p. 24.

71. H. de la Fontaine Verwey, 'Het Werk van de Blaeu's'. *Maandblad Amstelodamum*, 39 (1952), p. 102.